NANCY SILVERTON'S
SANDWICH BOOK

NANCY SILVERTON'S SANDWICH BOOK

The Best Sandwiches Ever—from Thursday Nights at Campanile

NANCY SILVERTON WITH TERI GELBER

PHOTOGRAPHS BY AMY NEUNSINGER

ALFRED A. KNOPF NEW YORK 2002

This Is a Borzoi Book Published by Alfred A. Knopf

Copyright © 2002 by Nancy Silverton
Photographs copyright © 2002 by Amy Neunsinger

All rights reserved under International and Pan-American Copyright
Conventions. Published in the United States by Alfred A. Knopf,
a division of Random House, Inc., New York, and simultaneously
in Canada by Random House of Canada Limited, Toronto.
Distributed by Random House, Inc., New York.
www.aaknopf.com

Library of Congress Cataloging-in-Publication Data

Silverton, Nancy.
Nancy Silverton's sandwich book : the best sandwiches ever—from
Thursday nights at Campanile /
Nancy Silverton with Teri Gelber;
photographs by Amy Neunsinger. — 1st ed.
p.   cm.

Includes index.
ISBN 0-375-41260-3 (alk. paper)
1. Sandwiches. I. Gelber, Teri. II. Title.
TX818 .S62 2002
641.8'4—dc21   2002019768

Manufactured in England

First Edition

TO THE MEMORY OF MY WONDERFUL MOTHER,
DORIS SILVERTON,
WHO ALWAYS REFUSED TO SLICE OFF THE CRUSTS
AND COULD NEVER REMEMBER THAT I LIKED
MY BREAD CUT ON THE DIAGONAL.
YOUR FINICKY DAUGHTER NOW KNOWS
YOU MADE YOUR SANDWICHES WITH LOVE.

CONTENTS

CLOSED-FACED SANDWICHES

SORT-OF SANDWICHES

TEA SANDWICHES

SANDWICH CAKES AND COOKIES

BAR SNACKS

SPREADS AND CONDIMENTS

BREADS

NANCY SILVERTON'S
SANDWICH BOOK

INTRODUCTION

Several years ago, I was invited by my friend Rolando Beramendi to be a guest on a food junket in Tuscany. As he led our group from town to town, we walked, talked, slept, and breathed food, in addition, of course, to eating it. A lot of it. After a week of dining in premier Tuscan restaurants and tasting the region's artisanal products, I was ready to go home, vowing that I would never eat again.

Our final stop on the tour was a small neighborhood crostini bar in Florence, Fuori Porta, where locals come in the evening to eat a simple meal of toasted bread with toppings, drink wines by the glass, and relax with their friends after work. As waiters passed by carrying platters of assorted sandwiches, my appetite quickly returned. Before I knew it, I too was drinking red wine and eating grilled bread rubbed with garlic and layered with prosciutto, arugula, and Parmesan, or with tuna, egg, and anchovies, and feeling very Italian.

When I returned home to Los Angeles, I went through serious food cravings. Not for *bistecca fiorentina,* not for *ribollita,* not for *gelati,* but for that perfect meal at Fuori Porta; those open-faced sandwiches turned out to be the highlight of my trip. I couldn't stop thinking about them. Simply constructed with fresh ingredients, their flavor combinations were bold and unforgettable. It's not as if I had never seen a sandwich before, but as an adult, I had never been so excited about eating one.

The only other time I was that obsessed with sandwiches was when I was 8 years old. My parents would take me to the Choo Choo Burger in the San Fernando Valley, where I always ordered the tuna sandwich. I could barely wait to grab it off the electric train (which circled the diner's countertop delivering the customers' orders) when it pulled to a stop in front of me. These days, however, I need more than just a gimmick and a bland tuna sandwich to satisfy me.

Too often, American sandwiches are just a quick and easy meal that rarely transcend their generic coffee-shop incarnation. Served with a mayonnaisey potato or macaroni salad and a few sweet-pickle chips, those sandwiches are okay, but usually too predictable. Don't get me wrong: every now and then, I love an ordinary corned beef on rye or a classic turkey club. But it took a trip to Italy to make me realize once again that a sandwich could be something worthy of an obsession. And what an obsession it became!

With no crostini bar in my neighborhood and no future junket to Italy on my calendar, how could I relive that Florentine experience? I could open a sandwich shop, but I already had one restaurant—Campanile, in Los Angeles—and I didn't want another. And so the only solution was to convert the bar at Campanile into my own Sandwich Night.

I chose Thursday nights to serve a seasonal menu of open-faced and closed-faced sandwiches in the bar and on the surrounding patio. Like a weekly cocktail party, Sandwich Night rapidly became the place where Angelenos gathered for wine, conversation, and a fix of their current favorite sandwiches, like Croque Monsieur; Clam Sandwich with Parmesan Breadcrumbs; or Braised Artichokes, Ricotta, and Mint Pesto with Pine-

Nut Currant Relish. Finally, the sandwich had a starring role in a fine-dining restaurant. It was comforting to know that so many others shared my enthusiasm. It wasn't long before customers were asking me for recipes so they could satisfy their cravings for my sandwiches more than one night a week.

Whether because of childhood memories or the comfort of certain ingredients combined together, everyone likes sandwiches. When vegetables, cheese, and meats are piled on top of bread, they take on a less formal quality. Although many of the sandwiches in this book have all the components of a complete meal—a protein, a starch, and at least one vegetable— they lack the stuffiness of a sit-down dinner. Convivial and inviting, these sandwiches are something to nibble at, converse over, and share with your friends.

Don't look at them as complicated sandwiches, but as satisfying entrées on bread. Aside from a simple green salad, nothing is needed to accompany them. Though some are more demanding to prepare and require extra steps and techniques, others come together with no cooking at all. For the more complex sandwiches, start making the components a day or two ahead. Cauliflower Purée with Browned Butter and Hazelnuts isn't a last-minute meal, but if you start a day before and have your components ready, assembling it takes no time at all. Others, such as the Classic Grilled Cheese or French Baguette with Butter and Prosciutto, call for only two or three ingredients and very little cooking at all, if any.

If you're willing to venture beyond the basic construction of a sandwich (just slapping two pieces of bread together with filling in the middle), then this book will expand your horizons and teach you more than just sandwich making. You can learn how to braise beans in the oven, char rapini in a skillet, sauté fresh clams, and make mayonnaise from scratch. These are methods and recipes that you will use for the rest of your cooking life.

Be creative and think outside of the "sandwich box." All of the sandwich components can be readily adapted to use in other recipes or served with other favorite dishes you make. Instead of mashed potatoes with your roast chicken, serve the cauliflower purée. Brandade without its sandwich counterparts, chickpeas and roast tomatoes, makes an unusual dip for a party. And long-cooked broccoli is so addictive, I love to eat it hot or cold, alone or as a side dish.

These sandwiches come in all sizes and shapes and flavors: large or small, minimal or overstuffed, savory or sweet. From the simple combinations such as grilled bread brushed with pesto, to the traditional closed-faced Grilled Cheese and its variations, to the layered, meal-style sandwiches like the Piled-High Pork, there's enough variety for everyone in the chapters ahead. Add some sugar and a little chocolate to the sandwich concept, and you can bake your way into the "Sandwich Cakes and Cookies" chapter. If you're not as obsessed with sandwiches as I am, you'll find lots of non-sandwiches to try in the "Bar Snacks" or "Sort-Of Sandwiches" chapters. And if you spend a little extra time making the tea sandwiches, your guests will be dazzled from the first look to the last bite.

INGREDIENTS AND TECHNIQUES

As a working mother, I am fully aware of scheduling constraints in the kitchen, and for those with more ambition than time, substitutions can certainly be made. High-quality commercial jars of roasted peppers, tapenades, pestos, imported tuna, and marinated artichokes can be found in well-stocked supermarkets and delis. There are also many restaurants and chefs packaging and marketing their own homemade pantry products. Though I usually prefer to make my own, tailoring the seasonings to my liking, if I do buy the commercial counterpart, I read the ingredients on the label to assure myself of the integrity of the product, avoiding the ones that contain artificial flavorings, garlic powder, MSG, or other "unsavory" ingredients.

With a few exceptions, all of the sandwiches call for a hearth-baked white or whole-wheat sourdough bread, both of which are available in most supermarkets or from your local bakery. For the home cook who insists on making everything from scratch, I've included a bread chapter that contains a few basic recipes that don't require the time-consuming sourdough-starter method. A few of the sandwiches call for a specialty bread such as a baguette, or walnut or olive bread, which are also available at neighborhood bakeries and most supermarkets. And, for the fanatic cook who wants to duplicate exactly what we do here at Campanile, you can always find more of my bread recipes in *Nancy Silverton's Breads from the La Brea Bakery*.

The amounts of the toppings and fillings that the recipes yield are, unless otherwise noted, enough for four sandwiches made on slices of bread about 4 inches wide by 7 inches long. To achieve that size, buy a 2-pound round or oval loaf, have it sliced into $\frac{1}{2}$-inch-thick slices, and use the wider, center slices for your sandwiches. If you decide to make your own bread, most of the sandwiches can be made on the Crusty White Loaf (see page 219). It yields a loaf with a smaller girth, so, to feed four and use up the amounts of toppings I call for in the sandwich recipe, you'll need to improvise. Cut the loaf into six slices for open-faced sandwiches and twelve slices for closed-faced sandwiches. Then cut the slices in half and give each person three halves.

For grilling the bread, I prefer to use a home-style panini machine, a two-sided grill that resembles a waffle iron. The heavy metal grills apply pressure and heat to both sides of the bread or sandwich at once. There's no flipping necessary, and you don't need to exert any extra pressure on the sandwiches as they grill. Turn the panini machine to high and allow it to heat up for 5–10 minutes. For the open-faced sandwiches, spread a thin layer of softened butter on both sides of the bread. For the closed-faced sandwiches, be sure to choose two slices of bread that are a perfect fit when placed together and spread a thin layer of softened butter on

the outer sides of the bread. If the sandwich is filled before grilling, assemble the ingredients and place the top slice of bread over them, aligning the slices of bread. Transfer the sandwiches or bread slices to the grill, placing them side by side without overcrowding them. (Most home-style panini grills have room for two sandwiches or two slices of bread.) Close the top grill and cook them for a few minutes, until the bread is lightly browned. This practical and easy-to-use machine is the fastest, most efficient method for making grilled sandwiches.

If you don't own a panini grill, other techniques work fine. You can achieve the same effect with the coffee-shop method, using a heavy-bottomed pan or, better yet, a well-seasoned cast-iron skillet with some Clarified Butter (see page 201). For cooking the bread for open-faced sandwiches, simply brush a little of the clarified butter over both sides of each slice, and lightly brown each side in the pan. For the closed-faced sandwiches, place a tablespoon or so of the clarified butter in the skillet and cook the assembled sandwich over medium heat, covered with a lid. When the bottom side turns golden brown, flip the sandwich over and move it around so it absorbs some of the butter around the edge of the skillet, adding more butter if necessary.

For grilling an open-faced sandwich on a charcoal or gas grill, brush the bread with olive oil and grill it for a few minutes on each side. When grilling a closed-faced sandwich, place a metal bowl over it to help the cheese-melting process. (At home, this technique probably isn't worth the trouble, but if you're picnick-ing or camping, a charcoal grill comes in handy for a quick and tasty outdoor meal.) And simplest of all, for any of the open-faced sandwiches, you can certainly just toast the bread in a good old-fashioned toaster.

Now that you're privy to all of my secrets, you can have your own sandwich night at home. But I hope that doesn't mean that you won't take a Thursday night off and drop by Campanile, where I'll be standing over my panini grill behind the bar. By then, who knows? I may have come up with a few new sandwiches for you to try.

OPEN-FACED
SANDWICHES

Whether it's a *tartine* under the Eiffel Tower in Paris, a *montadito* at a tapas bar in Spain, a *crostone* outside the city gates of Florence, or an open-faced sandwich on Thursday night at Campanile in Los Angeles, you're still eating the same thing: toasted bread with topping.

Technically, these aren't really sandwiches. Layered and stacked on a crisp bread pedestal, they're more closely related to the canapé. But whereas canapés call for the precise placement and rigid composition of fussy ingredients, these free-form assemblages are put together with ease. Never dainty or shy, they are proud sandwiches with a friendly, in-your-face attitude.

Concealing the toppings underneath a slice of bread would be a crime. Their artful layers of colorful patterns and rustic textures are part of what makes these open-faced sandwiches so irresistible. On one sandwich, hard-cooked eggs are quartered and nestled beside ruby-red tuna topped off with crispy strands of fried leeks. On another, rumpled slices of prosciutto provide a salty pillow for a soft poached egg to rest on. And savory chunks of bacon set the tempo for the olive-oil-braised beans and marinated greens on another open-faced sandwich.

For most of my open-faced sandwiches, I use a hearth-baked white or whole-wheat sourdough bread. However, to add another flavor component to a couple of the sandwiches, I call for a specialty bread. For the goat-cheese and marinated-fennel sandwich, walnut bread provides a sweet and nutty addition. An earthy olive bread is a classic match for the rare-seared tuna, braised leeks, hard-cooked egg, and tapenade. But if you can't find these flavored breads and you don't have time to make them, you'll still create a satisfying sandwich by substituting a simple sourdough loaf.

Keep in mind the beauty of imperfection when

you are assembling and adding the toppings to these rustic-style sandwiches. Whether it's a smooth aïoli or salsa romesco, or a chunkier topping like long-cooked broccoli, the ingredients should never be uniformly spread to cover the entire piece of bread. Rather, spoon the ingredients unevenly over the slice, mounding them into shapely piles and leaving the crust exposed.

For the sandwiches that don't need to be put in the oven, it's easier to assemble them directly on the plate that you're serving them on. As you build your sandwich, season as you go. A squeeze of fresh lemon juice over the fava-bean purée, a drizzling of olive oil over the watercress, or a pinch of salt over sliced mozzarella lends more flavor and depth to the entire sandwich. A spoonful of chopped herbs, a pinch of fleur de sel, a few grindings of fresh black pepper, or a shaving of cheese is the only crowning touch these open-faced sandwiches call for. For shaved cheese, choose a firm, assertive aged cheese. The recipes call for Parmigiano-Reggiano because it's excellent quality and readily available, but feel free to substitute for it other hard aged cheeses, such as Manchego, Grana Padano, Vermont's shepherd cheese, aged Gouda, Vela aged dry jack. To achieve wide paper-thin slices, start out with a sizable, uniform-sized chunk of cheese that lets you get a grip on it with one hand. (You won't use all of the wedge.) Using a semi-flexible paring knife, a vegetable peeler, or a cheese shaver, shave the cheese directly over the sandwiches.

Whether made with one ingredient or six, whether eaten with a knife and fork or picked up with your hands, these toasted breads with topping might just be the best thing you've ever tasted.

GRILLED GARLIC BREAD

The simplest of all of these open-faced sandwiches is grilled bread rubbed with a raw clove of sweet and pungent garlic. After the bread is grilled, rub a clove of garlic over it and cut it in half on the diagonal. In the summer, turn it into the Catalan dish pa amb tomaquet *by rubbing the grilled garlic toast with the cut side of a perfectly ripened tomato half. For a cheese version, spread a slice of grilled bread with your favorite soft, creamy cheese, such as a fresh goat cheese, Teleme, or any triple-cream brie.*

4 slices white or whole-wheat sourdough bread (or see page 219)
1 garlic clove, peeled

Grill the bread according to the directions on page 8. Rub one side of each slice of bread with the garlic, covering the whole surface once. The intensity of garlic varies, so taste the bread to see if it needs another stroke or two of garlic.

LEFTOVER LEG OF LAMB SANDWICH

Assuming you roasted this leg of lamb last night for dinner and assuming you saved about twelve ounces for leftovers, I assume you will want to make this sandwich.

Preheat the oven to 425 degrees.

Spread open the boneless leg of lamb, fat side down, on a work surface and sprinkle 2 tablespoons of the salt and the pepper and the paprika and oregano over the meat. Bring the long strip up to the middle section and fold the two side flaps over the middle to make a compact roast. Cut three 12-inch-long pieces of kitchen twine. Turn the meat over, so that it's seam side down, and sprinkle the remaining salt and pepper over it. Wrap a piece of the twine once around the center of the meat and tie it in a very tight knot. Wrap two more pieces of twine around the roast, placing them about 1 inch from each end.

Place a roasting rack on a baking sheet and place the lamb on the rack. Roast in the oven for about 1 hour and 30 minutes or until the lamb reaches an internal temperature of 125 degrees on a meat thermometer.

Using a very sharp knife or meat slicer, slice the leftover lamb (straight from the refrigerator) into paper thin slices. In a medium saucepan, over medium heat, bring the stock to a simmer.

TO ASSEMBLE THE SANDWICHES: Grill the bread according to the directions on page 8. Rub one side of each slice of bread with the garlic clove and place on serving plates, garlic side up. Scatter the arugula over the bread and place 2 slices of eggplant on top. Dip a few slices (about 3 ounces) of the lamb in the stock, swirling them around quickly for a few seconds only, so that you warm them up without cooking and discoloring them. Pile the lamb on top of the eggplant, spoon a tablespoon or two of pesto over it and crumble the feta over the top. Continue with the remaining sandwiches.

1 leg of lamb, bone removed
(about 5 pounds)
3 tablespoons kosher salt
3 tablespoons freshly cracked
black pepper
3 tablespoons Spanish paprika
3 tablespoons dried Greek oregano

4 slices white or whole-wheat
sourdough bread
1 garlic clove, peeled

2 cups beef, veal, or chicken stock,
homemade or the store-bought,
low-sodium variety
1 recipe Grilled Eggplant
(see page 39)
1 recipe Mint Pesto (see page 212)
Approximately 1 cup arugula,
loosely packed (about ½ ounce)
6 ounces Valbreso feta or
fresh goat cheese

CREMINI MUSHROOM TOASTS

On this simple sandwich, mushrooms are embedded in a linear pattern when grilled into the bread. To achieve this effect, you'll need a two-sided Italian-style panini machine. I prefer the brown button-variety mushrooms called Cremini for their earthy and deep flavors. Choose ones that are firm, dry, and fresh, completely closed around the base of the cap. If you can't find Cremini, use white domestic mushrooms instead.

12–16 Cremini mushrooms, bottom of stems trimmed
4 slices white or whole-wheat sourdough bread or brioche (or see page 219)
¼ cup extra-virgin olive oil
Kosher salt, to taste

Place the mushrooms on your work surface cap side down. Trim two sides off the caps in line with the stems (so that when you slice the mushrooms there will be no stemless slices).

Using a mandoline or a very sharp knife, cut the mushrooms into paper-thin slices, making sure to keep the stem section attached.

Brush one side of each slice of bread lightly with oil. Place the mushrooms in a row on the unoiled side of the bread, slightly overlapping, making 3 or 4 rows to cover the surface. (There should be about 18 slices total for each piece of bread with no gaps of bread showing through.) Dab the mushrooms with olive oil and sprinkle with salt.

Place the bread, mushroom side up, in a panini-style grill, and close the grill top over the bread, pressing the top of the grill down to slightly smash the bread. Grill for about 3 minutes on medium high, until the bread is golden brown and the mushrooms are sizzling and cooked through.

MARIO'S FAVORITE BAGNA CAUDA SANDWICH

I thought this chapter was done until my friend Mario Batali showed up in the piazza of the little Italian town where I vacation every summer. I made him an evening snack of grilled bread and hard-cooked egg bathed in a warm anchovy sauce. When he got back to New York, he called me and demanded, "You better put that recipe in your book!" Literally translated as "warm bath," bagna cauda has three of my favorite ingredients: garlic, olive oil, and anchovies.

If you happen to have any Sautéed Bitter Greens (see page 32), Long-Cooked Greens (see page 65), Braised Leeks (see page 27), or Roasted Radicchio (page 40), spoon some onto the bread in place of the arugula for a meal-style sandwich.

FOR THE BAGNA CAUDA: Using a mortar and pestle, pulverize the garlic and anchovies until a smooth paste.

Transfer the paste to a small saucepan. Add the butter and olive oil and bring to a simmer over low heat. Continue simmering for about 5 minutes. Remove the pan from the heat and stir in the lemon zest and lemon juice. Season with salt, to taste.

TO HARD-COOK THE EGGS: Place the eggs in a medium saucepan with water to cover. Bring to a boil over high heat and turn down to a low simmer. Simmer the eggs for 5 minutes, and immediately plunge them into a large bowl of ice water for a minute or so. Take them out as soon as they're cool.

Grill the bread according to the instructions on page 8. Rub one side of each slice of bread with the garlic clove, and slice the bread on the diagonal into thirds, to make triangles. Place the slices on serving plates, garlic side up.

TO ASSEMBLE THE SANDWICH: Arrange the arugula over each piece of bread. Cut the top ½ inch off the eggs and, using a spoon, scoop them out of their shells in large spoonfuls onto the bread. Drizzle 2–3 tablespoons of the warm bagna cauda over the top.

FOR THE BAGNA CAUDA

2–3 garlic cloves, peeled and finely chopped (about 1 tablespoon)

4 3-inch-long salt-packed anchovies, rinsed well, backbones removed, finely chopped (about 1 tablespoon)

1 stick (4 ounces) unsalted butter

½ cup extra-virgin olive oil

½ teaspoon finely chopped lemon zest

3–4 teaspoons fresh lemon juice, or to taste

Kosher salt, to taste

6 extra-large eggs

4 slices white or whole-wheat sourdough bread (or see page 219)

1 garlic clove, peeled

Approximately 2 cups arugula leaves, loosely packed (about 1 to 1½ ounces)

BREAKFAST SANDWICH

*To turn this breakfast sandwich into a midnight snack, skip the scallion oil and eggs.
Instead, grill a slice of bread, rub it with garlic, and layer it with prosciutto, arugula, and
shavings of Parmigiano-Reggiano.*

TO MAKE THE SCALLION OIL: In a food processor fitted with a metal blade, or with a mortar and pestle, process or pulverize the scallions and parsley until finely chopped. Add the olive oil and process or pulverize another few seconds to combine.

Grill the bread according to the directions on page 8. Rub one side of each slice of bread with the garlic clove, and place on serving plates, garlic side up.

TO POACH THE EGGS: In a medium saucepan, bring 2 quarts of water to a boil. Turn the heat down to just below a simmer and add the vinegar and salt. Crack an egg into a small bowl to check that the yolk isn't broken. Slowly stir the water in one direction to create a whirlpool effect. Once the whirlpool has slowed down a little, carefully slide the egg into the water against the side of the pan, following the current of the water as you pour the egg in, so that the white envelops the yolk. Crack another egg into the small bowl, and add to the water in the same manner. Poach the eggs for 2 to 2½ minutes, until the whites are set and the yolks are runny. Carefully remove with a slotted spoon to a plate to drain. Cupping the eggs in your hand, tip the plate to pour off the excess water. Poach the other 2 eggs in the same manner.

(If you want to prepare the eggs ahead of time, slip the poached eggs into a bowl of ice water and, just before assembling the sandwiches, return them to the simmering water for 10–20 seconds to warm.)

TO ASSEMBLE THE SANDWICHES: Spoon a tablespoon of scallion oil over the bread. Drape the prosciutto over it, and scatter the arugula. Center the poached egg over each slice of bread, and drizzle a teaspoon of scallion oil over the egg. Sprinkle the fleur de sel over.

FOR THE SCALLION OIL

1 bunch scallions, green parts only, coarsely chopped (about ⅓ cup)

⅓ cup coarsely chopped fresh Italian parsley leaves

½ cup extra-virgin olive oil

4 slices white or whole-wheat sourdough bread (or see page 219)

1 garlic clove, peeled

FOR THE EGGS

2 tablespoons white-wine vinegar

Pinch of kosher salt

4 extra-large eggs

Approximately 2 ounces prosciutto, thinly sliced into 8 pieces

Approximately 2 cups arugula leaves, loosely packed (about 1 to 1½ ounces)

Fleur de sel or kosher salt, to taste

ASPARAGUS, POACHED EGG, PROSCIUTTO, AND FONTINA CHEESE

This open-faced beauty gets my vote for the most visually appealing sandwich. Like a slightly sheer and slinky dress, this sandwich leaves more up to the imagination: the melted Fontina and rumpled slices of prosciutto conceal the good things to come.

TO ROAST THE ASPARAGUS: Adjust the oven rack to the middle position, and preheat the oven to 450 degrees.

To check the asparagus for tenderness, bite into the end. If it's stringy and tough, peel the outer layer of the bottom inch or two of each stalk. Place the asparagus in a large bowl, drizzle the olive oil over it, and sprinkle with salt, tossing to coat. Scatter 16 of the thyme sprigs onto a baking sheet and lay the asparagus stalks over them to cover. Roast in the oven for about 10 minutes, until tender to the touch yet firm in the center.

Grill the bread according to the directions on page 8. Rub one side of each slice of bread with the garlic clove, and place on a baking sheet, garlic side up.

Arrange the asparagus over each slice of bread and place on a baking sheet.

Adjust the oven rack to the upper position, and preheat the broiler.

TO POACH THE EGGS: In a medium saucepan, bring 2 quarts of water to a boil. Turn the heat down to just below a simmer and add the vinegar and salt. Crack an egg into a small bowl to check that the yolk isn't broken. Slowly stir the water in one direction to create a whirlpool effect. Once the whirlpool has slowed down a little, carefully slide the egg into the water against the side of the pan, following the current of the water as you pour the egg in, so that the white envelops the yolk. Crack another egg into the small bowl and add to the water in the same manner. Poach the eggs for 2 to 2½ minutes, until the whites are set and the yolks are runny. Carefully

FOR THE ASPARAGUS

16 to 20 stalks large or jumbo asparagus, tough ends broken off

1 tablespoon extra-virgin olive oil

½ teaspoon kosher salt

20 sprigs fresh thyme

4 slices white or whole-wheat sourdough bread (or see page 219)

1 garlic clove, peeled

FOR THE EGGS

2 tablespoons white-wine vinegar

Pinch of kosher salt

4 extra-large eggs

3 ounces Fontina or Gruyère cheese, sliced into 4 ⅛-inch-thick slices

2 ounces prosciutto di Parma, prosciutto di San Daniele, or Serrano ham, thinly sliced into about 8 slices

Extra-virgin olive oil, for drizzling over the sandwiches

Freshly cracked black pepper, to taste

remove with a slotted spoon to a plate to drain. Cupping the eggs in your hand, tip the plate to pour off the excess water.

Place the eggs centered over the asparagus. Poach the other 2 eggs in the same manner.

(If you want to prepare the eggs ahead of time, slip the poached eggs into a bowl of ice water, and just before assembling the sandwiches, return them to the simmering water for 10–20 seconds to warm.)

Drape a slice of Fontina cheese over each egg, and heat the sandwiches under the broiler for a minute or so, just until the cheese is melted.

Remove the sandwiches from the oven, and rumple a slice of prosciutto over each end of the asparagus, allowing the ends to peek out. Drizzle a little olive oil over, sprinkle with pepper, and place a thyme sprig on each sandwich.

Soft-Scrambled Eggs, Long-Cooked Broccoli, and Feta Cheese

Everyone has her nightmarish memories of Mom's boiled vegetables cooked into unappetizing shades of greenish gray. Some are scarred for life and won't go near anything cooked beyond the point of crisp and bright green. But there's a difference between long-cooked and overcooked. Stewed in olive oil, onion, and garlic for almost 2 hours, my long-cooked broccoli develops a deep, rich flavor unlike anything you've ever had before. Sweet and earthy at the same time, it is the perfect partner to the creamy and slightly salty feta cheese. This egg sandwich is delicious for any meal of the day, breakfast, lunch, or dinner.

TO COOK THE BROCCOLI: Cut the head of broccoli off the stalk, leaving about 1 inch of the stalk still attached. Slice the outer layer of fibrous peel off the main stalk, and cut it vertically into long, flat slices, about ¼ inch thick and 1 inch wide. (If the broccoli seems extra tough and fibrous, slice the stalk on the extreme diagonal into ¼-inch-thick pieces.) Slice all the way through the broccoli top, cutting it vertically into 1-inch-thick pieces, cutting through the florets when necessary. You should have several long pieces of broccoli.

In a large pot, bring 8 cups of water and ¼ cup of the salt to a boil. Cook all of the cut-up broccoli in the boiling water for about 2 minutes, until it turns bright green. Drain the pieces and place them in a large bowl of ice water to chill. Drain them well, and pat dry with a kitchen towel.

In a large heavy-duty skillet, combine the pieces of broccoli, garlic, onion, olive oil, chile, and 2 teaspoons salt. Over very low heat, cook the broccoli, stirring occasionally, for about 1½ hours, until it's very soft and tender. Season with salt, to taste.

Grill the bread according to the directions on page 8. Rub one side of each slice of bread with the garlic clove, and place the slices on serving plates, garlic side up.

TO SCRAMBLE THE EGGS: In a medium bowl, whisk 4 of the eggs with half of the salt. Melt the butter in a large non-stick skillet over medium heat. When the butter starts to bubble, pour the eggs into the pan. Using a heat-proof rubber spatula, scrape down the sides and bottom of the pan, letting the uncooked egg run underneath around the edges, folding the egg over itself, keeping it continuously moving. Cook about 2–3 minutes, until the egg is very softly scrambled with large curds. Repeat with the remaining eggs and salt.

TO ASSEMBLE THE SANDWICHES: Arrange the broccoli unevenly over the bread and squeeze a few drops of lemon juice over it. Pile the scrambled eggs on top, leaving a 1-inch border of broccoli around the edge. Sprinkle with salt and cracked black pepper, to taste. Crumble about 2 tablespoons feta on top of each, and sprinkle with chives.

FOR THE LONG-COOKED
BROCCOLI
1–2 heads broccoli (about 1¾ pounds), 1-inch end of stalk trimmed off
¼ cup plus 2 teaspoons kosher salt
4 garlic cloves, peeled and thinly sliced
1 small onion, thinly sliced
½ cup plus 2 tablespoons extra-virgin olive oil
1 whole dried red chile
4 slices white or whole-wheat sourdough bread (or see page 219)
1 garlic clove, peeled

FOR THE SCRAMBLED EGGS
8 extra-large eggs
½ teaspoon kosher salt
2 tablespoons unsalted butter

1–2 teaspoons fresh lemon juice, or to taste
Freshly cracked black pepper, to taste
4–6 ounces feta cheese, preferably French Valbreso or Bulgarian
¼ cup finely chopped fresh chives

CAULIFLOWER PURÉE WITH BROWNED BUTTER AND HAZELNUTS

This sandwich combination is a treat to myself. It makes up for all the years I wasted my appetite substituting an order of boring steamed cauliflower for the much tastier (and more fattening) creamed spinach. Though certain vegetables, such as carrots, beans, and peas, are delicious eaten raw or lightly steamed without extras, I think cauliflower demands a little more to bring out its best qualities. When cooked in cream and bathed in browned butter, cauliflower even puts creamed spinach to shame.

You'll need all of the cream to immerse the cauliflower when it's cooking; however, you probably won't need to use all of it when puréeing.

Adjust the oven rack to the middle position, and preheat the oven to 325 degrees.

Place the hazelnuts on a baking sheet, and toast in the oven for about 12 minutes, until lightly browned. Remove from the oven. Place them in a kitchen towel and rub them together between your palms to remove the skins. Chop coarsely and set aside.

Slice the stalk away from the head of the cauliflower. Break the large cauliflower florets into several small florets. Slice 4 or 5 of the florets into 32 ¼-inch-thick slices and set aside.

Slice the cauliflower stalk into ¼-inch-thick slices.

Place the small florets and sliced stem in a small saucepan, and pour the cream over to cover. Add the garlic cloves, onion, and 1 teaspoon of the salt, and bring to a boil over medium heat. Immediately turn down to a simmer and, stirring frequently, cook for about 30 minutes, until the cauliflower is very soft. Remove the pan from the heat, and allow to sit for 5 minutes. Strain, and reserve the cream.

Transfer three-quarters of the cooked cauliflower to a food mill or a food processor fitted with a metal blade. Add half of the cream back to the

¼ cup (1 ounce) hazelnuts

FOR THE CAULIFLOWER PURÉE

1 small head cauliflower (about 12 ounces), green leaves removed, and main stalk trimmed to about 1 inch below florets
1–2 cups heavy cream (depending on the size of pan)
2 garlic cloves, peeled
½ small yellow onion, thinly sliced
2 tablespoons plus 2 teaspoons kosher salt

FOR THE BREADCRUMBS

1 loaf white or whole-wheat sourdough bread (or see page 219) (Note: use the remaining half for the sandwich slices)
1 stick (4 ounces) unsalted butter
2 teaspoons kosher salt

4 slices white or whole-wheat sourdough bread (or see page 219) (see above)
1 garlic clove, peeled
1–2 teaspoons fresh lemon juice
12 sprigs fresh chervil, stems removed

cauliflower, and process it into a smooth purée. (The texture should be similar to creamy mashed potatoes.) If the mixture is too thick, add more of the cream and process it for a few more seconds. Save the remaining cream for another use.

Mash the remaining cauliflower with a fork until it's a coarse, chunky purée. Stir in the puréed cauliflower and 1 teaspoon of salt, or to taste.

In a medium saucepan, bring 6 cups of water and 2 tablespoons of salt to a boil. Cook the reserved uncooked cauliflower slices in the boiling water for about 1 minute to soften slightly. Drain, and transfer to a large bowl of ice water. As soon as they're cool, drain well.

TO MAKE THE BREADCRUMBS: Cut the loaf of bread in half and reserve half of the loaf to slice for the sandwiches. Using your fingers, reach in beneath the crust to pull out 1–2-inch pieces of the bread. Place them in a food processor fitted with the metal blade and process them into a fine meal, or use a knife to chop finely.

In a large skillet over medium heat, melt 3 tablespoons of the butter. When the butter is bubbling, add the cauliflower slices and sauté for 2–3 minutes on each side, until nicely browned. Remove with a slotted spoon.

Add the remaining butter to the skillet and, over medium heat, cook the butter for 2–3 minutes, until it's bubbly and brown. Add the breadcrumbs and salt, and cook until the breadcrumbs are toasted, about 2–3 minutes. Strain the breadcrumbs, and reserve the browned butter.

In a small saucepan, warm the cauliflower purée over very low heat for a few minutes, stirring frequently to ensure it doesn't burn.

Grill the bread according to the directions on page 8. Rub one side of each slice of bread with the garlic clove, and place on serving plates, garlic side up.

TO ASSEMBLE THE SANDWICH: Spoon the cauliflower purée unevenly over the bread. Arrange the cauliflower pieces on top, and sprinkle with breadcrumbs. Pour the browned butter over the sandwiches, and scatter the hazelnuts on top. Squeeze a few drops of lemon juice, to taste, and garnish with chervil.

RARE-SEARED TUNA,
BRAISED LEEKS,
HARD-COOKED EGG,
AND TAPENADE

Although mothers aren't supposed to play favorites, this sandwich might be mine. It may seem overwhelming, with lots to prepare—whisking the aïoli, braising the leeks, searing the tuna, and making the tapenade. And if that's not enough for you, you have the option of frying leeks to top off the sandwich. As in any other multi-step recipe, the more you do ahead of time, the better. Each of these components can be made a day or so early.

TO BRAISE THE LEEKS: Adjust the oven rack to the middle position, and preheat the oven to 450 degrees.

Peel away the outer layer of the leek. Place the leek on the cutting board with the white end pointing away from you. To remove the dark-green part of the leek, slice a section of it off at an angle. Roll the leek a quarter-turn and repeat the same cut. Continue rolling and slicing a few more times in this manner until the tapered pale-green end resembles a sharpened pencil. Discard the dark-green trimmings.

Cut the leeks in half lengthwise, rinse to remove the fine grit, and pat dry. Place the leeks, olive oil, and salt in a 9-by-13-inch baking dish (it is important that they fit snugly). Pour in the chicken stock, and arrange the lemon slices over the leeks. Cover tightly with plastic wrap and then foil, and braise for about 35–40 minutes in the oven. Remove the foil, puncture the plastic to allow the steam to escape, and then remove the plastic.

Return the dish to the oven, and bake for another 30–45 minutes, until the leeks are tender, shiny, and caramelized and the liquid is reduced. If there is a lot of liquid left, remove the leeks and transfer the liquid to a small saucepan. Over medium-high heat, reduce the liquid until slightly thickened. Pour over the leeks. If you're not using the leeks that day, you can refrigerate

FOR THE BRAISED LEEKS
4 leeks, root ends trimmed
2 tablespoons extra-virgin olive oil
¼ teaspoon kosher salt
1½ cups chicken stock, homemade
or store-bought low-sodium variety
1 lemon, cut into ⅛-inch-thick slices

FOR THE TUNA
1 tablespoon fennel seeds
1 tablespoon cumin seeds
1 tablespoon coriander seeds
2 teaspoons caraway seeds
2 teaspoons cracked black peppercorns
2 teaspoons kosher salt
12 ounces ahi (yellowfin) tuna, cut
into a roughly 2-by-4-inch block
1 tablespoon vegetable oil

4 extra-large eggs

1 recipe Aïoli (see page 204)

FOR THE FRIED LEEKS
(OPTIONAL)
2 leeks, root ends trimmed,
and dark-green section cut
off and discarded
Vegetable oil, for frying

them and rewarm them in the oven before assembling the sandwiches.

FOR THE TUNA: In a small cast-iron or heavy-duty skillet, toast the fennel seeds, cumin seeds, coriander seeds, and caraway seeds for about 3–4 minutes over medium-high heat, until they release their aromas. Combine the black pepper with the spices and coarsely grind them in a spice grinder or a mortar and pestle.

Salt the tuna on each side. Spread the spices out on a plate and press each side of the tuna into the ground spices, so that it's evenly coated.

In the same skillet, heat the oil over high heat. When the oil is very hot and almost smoking, sear the tuna on each side for about 30 seconds. Refrigerate until cold. Cut it into 16 slices just under ¼ inch thick.

TO HARD-COOK THE EGGS: Place the eggs in a small saucepan with water to cover. Bring them to a boil over high heat, then turn the heat down to a low simmer. Simmer for 7 minutes, and immediately plunge the eggs into a large bowl of ice water to chill.

FOR THE DEEP-FRIED LEEKS: Slice the leeks in half lengthwise, and cut into thirds crosswise. Slice each section into very fine, long strands. Rinse under cold water, drain, and pat dry.

In a deep heavy-duty saucepan, heat the oil to 350 degrees on a deep-fat-frying thermometer. Fry the leek strands in the oil, stirring constantly. Remove them as soon as they begin to change color and darken slightly. Drain on paper towels.

Grill the bread according to the directions on page 8. Rub one side of each slice of bread with the garlic clove, and place garlic side up.

Spread about 2 tablespoons of the aïoli unevenly over the bread. Cut each slice in half on the diagonal, and place on serving plates.

Peel the eggs and cut into quarters.

TO ASSEMBLE THE SANDWICH: Cut the leeks in half horizontally at an angle. Place a half over each piece of bread, fanning it out slightly. Arrange the slices of tuna on the diagonal over the leeks and place two quarters of an egg on each half. Spoon about half a teaspoon of the tapenade over each piece of egg. If you're using fried leeks, arrange them over the top. Sprinkle the sandwiches with the chives and fleur de sel.

4 slices olive, white, or whole-wheat
sourdough bread (or see page 219)
1 garlic clove, peeled

About 3 tablespoons Tapenade
(see page 211)
Approximately 1 bunch
chives, minced
Fleur de sel or kosher salt, to taste

CHOPPED "SUB"

Mention the restaurant La Scala to anyone from Los Angeles and the words "chopped salad" will undoubtedly follow. That combination of shredded iceberg, salami, cheese, and garbanzos drenched in Eye-talian dressing was one of my favorite meals growing up. I finally have an excuse to turn that famous Beverly Hills dish into a chopped submarine sandwich.

TO MAKE THE VINAIGRETTE: In a bowl, whisk together the lemon juice, vinegar, oregano, garlic, oils, salt, and cracked black pepper. Season with more lemon juice, salt, and pepper, to taste.

Slice the salami and cheese into ⅛-inch-wide matchsticks.

If you're using Sweet 100's, cut them in half. If you're using cherry tomatoes, cut them into quarters. If you're using large tomatoes, cut them in half, scrape out the seeds, and chop into ½-inch dice. No matter which kind of tomato you're using, the amount should equal about 1½ cups cut or chopped.

In a large bowl, combine the salami, provolone cheese, tomatoes, radicchio, iceberg lettuce, and chickpeas.

Pour half of the vinaigrette over the salad, and toss well.

Grill the bread according to the directions on page 8. Rub one side of each slice of bread with the garlic clove, and place on serving plates, garlic side up.

Pile the tossed salad over each slice of bread. Crumble the blue cheese over the salad, and sprinkle a pinch of oregano on top. Spoon a little of the remaining vinaigrette over the salad and around the edges of the bread. Serve the pepperoncini on the side.

1 recipe Chickpeas (see page 50), cooled and drained

FOR THE OREGANO VINAIGRETTE

2 teaspoons fresh lemon juice

1 tablespoon red-wine vinegar

2 teaspoons dried oregano, plus extra for sprinkling on the sandwiches

1 garlic clove, peeled and finely chopped (about 1 teaspoon)

¼ cup vegetable oil

¼ cup extra-virgin olive oil

¾ teaspoon kosher salt

Freshly cracked black pepper, to taste

4 ounces Italian salami, sliced ⅛ inch thick

4 ounces provolone cheese, preferably aged, sliced ⅛ inch thick

1 pint Sweet 100's or cherry tomatoes, or 1–2 large tomatoes (about 10 ounces)

½ medium head radicchio, finely chopped (about 2 cups)

About 4½ cups finely shredded iceberg lettuce, about 1 small head

4 slices white or whole-wheat sourdough bread (or see page 219)

1 garlic clove, peeled

2 ounces Roquefort or other blue cheese

8 pepperoncini

BRAISED LEEKS,
HARD-COOKED EGG,
AND ANCHOVIES

If you think you've already seen the combination of braised leeks, hard-cooked egg, and fish in this book, you're right. If you think that the two versions—this one with anchovy, the other with tuna—taste the same, you're wrong. Put the two side by side, close your eyes, and take a bite. See, they're completely different experiences; it's the salty kick and dense meaty texture of the anchovies that set these two sandwiches worlds apart.

1 recipe Braised Leeks, (see page 27)

1 recipe Aïoli (see page 204)

8 3-inch salt-packed anchovies, rinsed well and backbone removed

¼ cup extra-virgin olive oil

½ lemon, zested into long strands

1 tablespoon finely chopped fresh Italian parsley

4 extra-large eggs

4 slices white or whole-wheat sourdough bread (or see page 219)

1 garlic clove, peeled

TO MARINATE THE ANCHOVIES: In a small bowl, combine the anchovy fillets, olive oil, lemon zest, and parsley and toss to coat the fish. Allow to sit at room temperature for at least 1 hour.

TO HARD-COOK THE EGGS: Place the eggs in a medium saucepan with water to cover. Bring to a boil over high heat and turn down to a low simmer. Simmer the eggs for 7 minutes and immediately plunge them into a large bowl of ice water to chill.

Peel the eggs and cut them into quarters.

Grill the bread according to the directions on page 8. Rub one side of each slice of bread with the garlic and place garlic side up.

TO ASSEMBLE THE SANDWICHES: Spread about 2 tablespoons of the aïoli unevenly over the bread. Cut each slice of bread in half on the diagonal and place them on serving plates.

Cut the leeks in half horizontally at an angle and place them over each half-slice of bread, fanning the leeks out slightly. Place 2 quarters of an egg over each leek. Drape an anchovy fillet over each egg quarter and drizzle with some of the anchovy marinade.

PEPPERED BEEF,
SAUTÉED BITTER GREENS,
AND CAPER ONION
MAYONNAISE

What's a sandwich book without a steak sandwich? My steak is seared with four types of peppercorns, sliced, then pounded thin, sauced with a tasty caper mayonnaise, and, if you like, topped with crunchy deep-fried capers.

You can find Szechuan peppercorns in Asian or Indian markets.

FOR THE BEEF: Salt the filet on all sides.

Spread the ground peppercorns on a plate and stir to combine. Press each side of the filet into the pepper, so that it's evenly coated.

In a small cast-iron or heavy-duty skillet, heat the vegetable oil over high heat. When the oil is very hot and almost smoking, sear the beef about a minute on each side. Refrigerate until cold. Using a sharp knife, slice the beef, against the grain, into 16 ¼-inch-thick slices. Brush both sides of each slice with olive oil, and place them all between 2 sheets of plastic wrap. Using the flat side of a mallet or a meat tenderizer, gently pound each piece until it's ⅛ inch thick.

TO SAUTÉ THE GREENS: In a large skillet over medium-high heat, heat a teaspoon or so of the oil until very hot but not smoking. Add the radicchio and cook about 2 minutes, until it's wilted. Add ¼ teaspoon of the chopped garlic, and cook another minute or two. Sprinkle in ¼ teaspoon of the salt and a few grindings of cracked black pepper, and add ½ teaspoon of the vinegar. Transfer the greens to a bowl. Wipe out the skillet, and continue in the same manner (adjusting the cooking time if necessary) for the endive, arugula, and frisée (in 3 separate batches). Toss the cooked greens together in the bowl, and season with salt and pepper, to taste.

1 recipe Caper Onion Mayonnaise
(see page 206)

FOR THE BEEF
4 ounces filet of beef or filet mignon
1 teaspoon kosher salt
1½ tablespoons coarsely ground
green peppercorns
1½ tablespoons coarsely ground
pink peppercorns
1½ tablespoons coarsely ground
black peppercorns
1½ tablespoons coarsely ground
Szechuan peppercorns
1 tablespoon vegetable oil
Extra-virgin olive oil, for brushing
on the meat

FOR THE GREENS
2 tablespoons vegetable oil
1 medium head radicchio (about
10 ounces), roughly chopped
into 1-inch squares
1–2 garlic cloves, peeled and finely
chopped (about 2 teaspoons)
1 teaspoon kosher salt
Freshly cracked black pepper, to taste

Fill a small saucepan with about an inch of oil, and over medium heat, bring the oil up to 350 degrees, measuring the temperature with a deep-fat-frying thermometer. Add the capers, and fry for about 1 minute, until they burst. Using a slotted spoon, transfer them to a paper towel to drain.

Grill the bread according to the directions on page 8. Rub one side of each slice of bread with the garlic clove, and place garlic side up.

TO ASSEMBLE THE SANDWICHES: Spread about 2 tablespoons of the caper mayonnaise unevenly over each slice of bread. Cut the bread in half on the diagonal, and place on serving plates.

Arrange the greens unevenly over the bread, and rumple 2 slices of beef over each half. Drizzle them with olive oil, and sprinkle on the capers. If you're not using capers, sprinkle the sandwiches with fleur de sel.

2 teaspoons balsamic vinegar

1 Belgian endive (about 6 ounces), most of the stem removed, sliced in half horizontally and roughly chopped

Approximately 8 cups arugula leaves, loosely packed (about 4 to 5 ounces)

1 large head frisée (about 4 ounces), center core removed, pulled apart into small bunches

FOR THE FRIED CAPERS (OPTIONAL)

Vegetable oil, for deep-frying

24 capers, preferably salt-packed, rinsed well and drained

4 slices white or whole-wheat sourdough bread (or see page 219)

1 garlic clove, peeled

Extra-virgin olive oil, for drizzling on the sandwiches

Fleur de sel or kosher salt, to taste (optional)

EGGPLANT, SEARED TUNA, AND ANCHOÏADE

The tuna in this sandwich can be prepared in two ways. If you want to take a fantasy trip to Provence, sear the tuna and slather it with anchoïade, an anchovy mayonnaise. If North Africa is more your style, marinate the tuna in chermoula and serve it with aïoli. Either way, you can never go wrong with tuna, eggplant, and mayonnaise.

FOR THE PROVENÇAL TUNA: In a small cast-iron or heavy-duty skillet, toast the fennel seeds, cumin seeds, coriander seeds, and caraway seeds for about 3–4 minutes over medium-high heat, until they begin to release their aromas. Combine the black pepper with the spices and coarsely grind them in a spice grinder or a mortar and pestle.

Salt the tuna on each side. Spread the spices out on a plate. Press each side of the tuna into the ground spices, so that it's evenly coated.

In the same skillet, heat the oil over high heat. When the oil is very hot and almost smoking, sear the tuna on each side for about 30 seconds. Refrigerate until cold and slice the tuna into 16 ¼-inch-thick slices.

FOR THE CHERMOULA TUNA: In a small cast-iron or heavy-duty skillet, toast the cumin seeds and fennel seeds for about 3–4 minutes over medium-high heat, until they begin to release their aromas. Finely grind them in a spice grinder or a mortar and pestle.

Place the garlic, ground cumin and fennel, paprika, and cayenne pepper in a mortar and pulverize them into a smooth paste. Or put them in a bowl, and stir to combine. Add the parsley, cilantro, mint, vinegar, lemon juice, salt, pepper, and olive oil, and stir to combine. Adjust the seasoning, to taste. Set aside about 4 tablespoons of the marinade to spoon over the fish after it's cooked. Place the tuna in the bowl or mortar, and marinate it for about 2 hours. Then sear and slice it in the same manner as the Provençal tuna. Drizzle the remaining 4 tablespoons of chermoula over the sliced tuna.

12 ounces ahi (yellowfin) tuna, cut into a 2-by-4-inch block

FOR THE PROVENÇAL-STYLE TUNA
2 tablespoons fennel seeds
2 tablespoons cumin seeds
2 tablespoons coriander seeds
1 tablespoon caraway seeds
1 tablespoon cracked black peppercorns
1 tablespoon kosher salt
2 tablespoons vegetable oil, for searing the tuna

FOR THE NORTH AFRICAN CHERMOULA TUNA
1 tablespoon cumin seeds
1 teaspoon fennel seeds
2 garlic cloves, finely chopped
1 tablespoon sweet paprika
1 teaspoon cayenne pepper
¼ cup finely chopped fresh Italian parsley leaves
¼ cup finely chopped fresh cilantro leaves
¼ cup finely chopped fresh mint leaves
2 teaspoons red-wine vinegar
2 teaspoons fresh lemon juice
1 teaspoon kosher salt
Freshly cracked black pepper, to taste

TO PREPARE THE EGGPLANT: Preheat your grill, panini machine, or skillet. Using a mandoline or sharp knife, slice the eggplant into long, paper-thin slices, and brush with olive oil. On a grill or in a skillet, cook the eggplant for 1 minute on each side until softened and slightly browned. In a panini machine, grill the eggplant for about 1 minute.

Grill the bread according to the directions on page 8. Rub one side of each slice of bread with the garlic clove, and place garlic side up.

TO ASSEMBLE THE SANDWICHES: Spread 2 tablespoons of anchoïade or aïoli (depending upon which tuna you make) unevenly over each slice of bread. Cut the bread in half on the diagonal, and place on serving plates.

Rumple 2 slices of the eggplant over each half, folding it over onto itself to fit on the bread. Place 2 slices of the tuna diagonally over each half. Sprinkle with the parsley leaves and fleur de sel.

½ cup extra-virgin olive oil

2 tablespoons vegetable oil, for searing the tuna

1 recipe Anchoïade (see page 205) if you're making the Provençal-Style Tuna or 1 recipe Aïoli (see page 204) if you're making the North African Chermoula Tuna

1–2 Japanese eggplants

2 tablespoons extra-virgin olive oil

4 slices white or whole-wheat sourdough bread (or see page 219)

1 garlic clove, peeled

2 tablespoons finely chopped fresh Italian parsley leaves

Fleur de sel or kosher salt, to taste

ROASTED BEETS, GOAT CHEESE, SAUTÉED BEET GREENS, AND CANDIED SPICY WALNUTS

You'll find some form of this combination on most California restaurant menus. The earthy beets, tangy goat cheese, and salty, spicy, and sweet nuts make it a well-rounded medley of flavors and textures.

If you don't have a salty-spicy-sweet tooth, skip the candied nuts and simply toast a few walnuts in the oven. One bunch of beets won't give you enough greens for all four sandwiches, so you'll either have to make a friend at the farmers' market, grow a row of beets in your garden and snip off the greens, buy extra beets and use them for something else, or substitute a couple of bunches of red chard instead.

TO PREPARE THE BEETS: Adjust the oven rack to the middle position, and preheat the oven to 350 degrees.

Place the beets in a large bowl. Add the thyme, 1 tablespoon of the olive oil, half of the salt, and pepper, and toss to coat the beets. Transfer to a baking dish large enough so that the beets are all in one layer. Add a splash of water and cover the dish tightly with plastic wrap and then foil, and roast the beets for about 40 minutes to an hour, until they're tender.

Remove the foil, puncture the plastic to allow the steam to escape, and then remove the plastic. Allow the beets to cool, and slip the skins off by hand. Cut each beet into 5 wedges about ½ inch thick.

In a large bowl, combine the shallots, vinegar, the remaining salt, pepper, and remaining oil. Toss the wedges of beets in the marinade, and set aside for at least 30 minutes.

TO PREPARE THE BEET GREENS: In a large pot, bring 8 cups of water and ¼ cup of salt to a boil. (If the beet greens are large, remove the stems

FOR THE MARINATED BEETS

4 medium beets (about 5 ounces),
ends trimmed

1 teaspoon finely chopped
fresh thyme leaves

¼ cup extra-virgin olive oil

1 teaspoon kosher salt

Freshly cracked black pepper, to taste

2 shallots, peeled and finely chopped
(about 3 tablespoons)

2 tablespoons red-wine vinegar

Approximately ½ recipe Candied
Spicy Walnuts (see page 192) or
8 walnut halves, toasted

FOR THE SAUTÉED GREENS

¼ cup kosher salt

4–5 bunches beet greens (about 1¼
pounds), or 2 bunches
red Swiss chard

¼ cup extra-virgin olive oil

2 shallots, peeled and thinly sliced

Kosher salt, to taste

Freshly cracked black pepper, to taste

and center ribs and prepare in same manner as the chard.) Cook the greens in the boiling water (in 2 batches) for about 1 minute, until wilted. Drain them, and place in a large bowl of ice water to chill. Drain well, and squeeze out the excess water.

TO PREPARE THE CHARD: In a large pot, bring 8 cups of water and $\frac{1}{4}$ cup of salt to a boil. Remove the stems and center ribs of the chard and slice them on the diagonal into 1-inch-thick pieces. Cook the stems and ribs for 2 minutes in the boiling water, remove them with a slotted spoon, and place in a large bowl of ice water to cool. Cook the chard leaves in the boiling water (in 2 batches) for about 1 minute, until wilted. Drain and place in a large bowl of ice water to cool. Drain well, and squeeze out the excess water.

In a large sauté pan over medium-high heat, heat the olive oil until hot but not smoking. Add the beet greens and shallots, and cook for about 3–4 minutes, stirring frequently. (If you're using chard, sauté the ribs for about 2 minutes, until just tender. Then add the leaves and shallots, and cook for about 3–4 minutes.) Season with salt and pepper, to taste.

Preheat the oven to 450 degrees.

Grill the bread according to the directions on page 8. Rub one side of each slice of bread with the garlic clove, and place on a baking sheet, garlic side up.

TO ASSEMBLE THE SANDWICHES: Arrange the greens and ribs unevenly over each slice of bread. Center the goat-cheese discs over the greens. Tuck 5 wedges of beets into the greens, 2 on one side of the goat cheese and 3 on the other. Heat the sandwiches in the oven for about 3–5 minutes, until the goat cheese is soft and warm but not melted.

Remove the sandwiches from the oven, and transfer them to serving plates. Place 2 walnut halves on each sandwich, and drizzle them all with a little walnut oil or olive oil.

4 slices white or whole-wheat sourdough bread (or see page 219)
1 garlic clove, peeled
1 small fresh goat-cheese log
(about 4 ounces), sliced into
½-inch-thick discs
Walnut oil or extra-virgin olive oil,
for drizzling on the sandwiches

GRILLED EGGPLANT, RICOTTA SALATA, AND GREENS

Just because this is one of the quickest sandwiches in the book to make doesn't mean it isn't one of the tastiest. Thin slices of smoky grilled eggplant piled with greens and topped with a salted, dried ricotta makes this the perfect light meal.

TO MAKE THE VINAIGRETTE: In a small mixing bowl, whisk together the vegetable oil, walnut oil, vinegar, and shallot. Season with salt and pepper, to taste.

TO PREPARE THE EGGPLANT: Preheat your grill, panini machine, or skillet. Using a mandoline or sharp knife, slice the eggplant into long, paper-thin slices and brush with olive oil. On a grill or in a skillet, cook the eggplant for 1 minute on each side, until softened and slightly browned. In a panini machine, grill the eggplant about 1 minute.

In a large bowl, toss the greens with the vinaigrette and season with salt and pepper to taste.

Grill the bread according to the directions on page 8. Rub one side of each slice of bread with the garlic clove, and place the slices on serving plates, garlic side up.

TO ASSEMBLE THE SANDWICHES: Pile the greens over the bread. Rumple 3 or 4 slices of the eggplant over each, folding them over themselves to fit on the bread. Place 4 or 5 slices of cheese over the eggplant, drizzle with olive oil, and sprinkle with pepper.

⅓ cup vegetable oil

3 tablespoons walnut oil

¼ cup plus 1 tablespoon
balsamic vinegar

1 shallot, finely chopped
(about 1 tablespoon)

Kosher salt, to taste

Freshly cracked black pepper, to taste

1–2 Japanese eggplants

2 tablespoons extra-virgin olive oil

Approximately 4 cups mesclun
salad mix, loosely packed
(about 2 to 3 ounces)

4 slices white or whole-wheat sourdough bread (or see page 219)

1 garlic clove, peeled

6 ounces ricotta salata, sliced
into paper-thin slices

Extra-virgin olive oil, for drizzling
on the sandwiches

Freshly cracked black pepper, to taste

Mozzarella, Pesto, and Roasted Radicchio

David Greco at Mike's Deli in the Bronx was shocked to find out how ignorant I was about storing fresh mozzarella. "Everyone knows that when freshly made mozzarella is to be eaten within a day or two it shouldn't be refrigerated!" When kept at room temperature, the super-fresh mozzarella maintains its soft, creamy texture and sweet, nutty flavor. Don't confuse the hard and rubbery, shrink-wrapped supermarket mozzarella with its fresh counterpart. That cheese has nothing in common with the tender, hand-pulled delicacy.

If you don't have a local mozzarella maker, buy mozzarella balls floating in whey from an upscale market or cheese store and keep them in the refrigerator. According to David, if you immerse the chilled balls in a bath of warm salted water just before serving, they'll soften into a tender, creamy consistency, closer in style to his handmade mozzarella.

I'm well aware that not everyone loves radicchio as much as I do. On this sandwich, I tried to temper its bitter sharpness by pairing it with a mild mozzarella. Now, if that still doesn't work for you, go for the more classic combo and substitute tomatoes for the radicchio. But do me a favor and only use tomatoes in season, and do yourself a favor and seek out colorful heirloom varieties, such as Cherokee Purple, Earl of Edgecombe, Brandywine, Black Krim, or Costeluto Fiorentino.

FOR THE RADICCHIO
1 medium head radicchio
(about 10 ounces),
cut in half through the core
3 tablespoons extra-virgin olive oil,
plus extra to drizzle over sandwiches
1 tablespoon balsamic vinegar
Approximately 2 branches fresh
rosemary, picked into 20 small sprigs
½ teaspoon kosher salt

1 recipe Basil Pesto (see page 212)

1 pound (2 large balls)
fresh mozzarella
2 cups warm water (optional)
1 tablespoon kosher salt (optional)

4 slices white or whole-wheat sourdough bread (or see page 219)
1 garlic clove, peeled

TO ROAST THE RADICCHIO: Adjust the oven rack to the middle position, and preheat the oven to 400 degrees.

Cut each radicchio half into 5 wedges. In a cast-iron or other ovenproof 10-inch skillet, combine 2 tablespoons of the olive oil and 2 teaspoons of the vinegar. Arrange the wedges of radicchio in the skillet in a concentric circle, and place a small piece of rosemary underneath and on top of each wedge.

Drizzle the remaining olive oil and vinegar over the radicchio, and sprinkle over the salt. Cover with plastic wrap and then foil, and roast in the oven for 15 minutes. Remove the foil, puncture the plastic to allow the steam to escape, and remove the plastic.

Turn the wedges of radicchio over, and on the stovetop, over medium heat, cook the radicchio about 3–5 minutes to caramelize slightly, being careful not to burn it.

TO SOAK THE MOZZARELLA: Bring it to room temperature and slice into ½-inch-thick slices. Pour warm salted water over the cheese to cover, and allow to sit a few minutes, until softened. Drain the slices on paper towels.

Grill the bread according to the directions on page 8. Rub one side of each slice of bread with the garlic clove, and cut each slice in half on the diagonal. Place the slices on serving plates, garlic side up.

TO ASSEMBLE THE SANDWICHES: Arrange 2 or 3 slices of mozzarella over each half-slice of bread, and spoon about a tablespoon of pesto over the cheese. Arrange the radicchio over the pesto and drizzle with olive oil.

FRIED PEQUILLO PEPPERS, BURRATA CHEESE, AND CRISP GARLIC

Finding a decent roasted-red-pepper-and-mozzarella sandwich in my neighborhood in Los Angeles was never difficult. Just about every Italian deli has its version. But creating a twist on the classic sandwich called for two trips to two different countries. I don't know if I would have ever thought to buy canned roasted peppers and fry them if I hadn't tasted them done in this manner at the "all-canned" lunch I ate in Spain. Frying the already roasted peppers in olive oil intensifies their flavor even more. And before I visited Puglia, I had never met mozzarella's more decadent cousin, Burrata. Its rich, buttery core is enveloped by a skin of mozzarella for a creamy, melt-in-your-mouth cheese that is rare but worth searching for.

Pequillo peppers are available in most upscale markets and through mail-order catalogues (see sources). Burrata, though a little harder to come by, can be found in good cheese stores or some Italian delis. For both of these seemingly exotic components, their more readily available counterparts can be substituted: homemade or store-bought roasted red bell peppers and standard fresh mozzarella.

3 or 4 garlic cloves, cut into about 20 paper-thin slices total

¾ cup extra-virgin olive oil

8 jarred or canned Pequillo peppers (approximately 6 ounces), or

1 8-ounce jar roasted red peppers, or

2 large roasted red bell peppers (see page 143)

1 teaspoon sugar

1 pound (3–4 balls) Burrata or fresh mozzarella cheese

Kosher salt, to taste

4 slices white or whole-wheat sourdough bread (or see page 219)

1 garlic clove, peeled

8–16 whole fresh basil leaves

TO FRY THE GARLIC: Place the garlic slices in a small saucepan with cold water to cover, and bring to a boil over medium heat. Drain the garlic, return it to the saucepan, and cover with cold water again. Bring to a boil and remove from the heat. Drain well and pat dry.

In the same small saucepan, over medium-high heat, warm ¼ cup of the olive oil until just below a boil. Fry the garlic slices a minute or two, stirring constantly (being careful not to burn them), until they're a pale-golden color. Remove immediately with a slotted spoon, and drain on paper towels. Reserve the oil for frying the peppers.

TO FRY THE PEPPERS: In a 10-inch skillet, warm the remaining garlic oil, the remaining ½ cup of olive oil, and the sugar over medium-high heat, until very hot, but not smoking. Fry the peppers for about 4 minutes on each side. Remove from the oil and allow to cool.

Cut the Burrata into ½-inch-thick slices. If you're using mozzarella, bring it to room temperature and slice it into ½-inch-thick slices; pour warm salted water over the cheese to cover, and allow it to sit a few minutes, until softened; drain the slices on paper towels.

Grill the bread according to the directions on page 8. Rub one side of each slice of bread with the garlic clove, and cut in half on the diagonal. Place the slices on serving plates, garlic side up.

TO ASSEMBLE THE SANDWICHES: Center 2 or 3 slices of cheese over each half-slice of bread, and spoon a teaspoon or so of the pepper oil over them. Place 2–4 basil leaves over the cheese, allowing the leaves to hang over the edge. Slice the Pequillo pepper open and rumple it on top of the cheese, on a diagonal. (If you're using roasted red bell peppers, cut them into quarters after roasting and use about 2 quarters per sandwich.) Drizzle a little more of the oil, and distribute the garlic slices on top.

Bacon, Avocado, and Watercress

Reminiscent of a BLT, this sandwich welcomes in the spring and takes you into early summer, before T's are in their prime.

Adjust the oven rack to the middle position, and preheat the oven to 350 degrees. Arrange the bacon on a baking sheet, and cook in the oven for about 20 minutes, until cooked all the way through but not crisp. Drain it on paper towels.

Place the avocado halves cut side down and slice lengthwise into ⅛-inch-thick slices. Press down gently on the halves to fan the slices out just a bit, keeping them intact.

Place the onion half cut side down and cut into paper-thin slices, keeping the slices intact.

Grill the bread according to the directions on page 8. Rub one side of each slice of bread with the garlic clove, and place on serving plates, garlic side up.

TO ASSEMBLE THE SANDWICHES: Spread 2 tablespoons of the green-goddess dressing unevenly over each slice of bread.

Arrange 3 pieces of bacon over each slice of bread, allowing the ends of the bacon to stick out over the edge of the bread. Pile the watercress on top, drizzle some lemon juice and olive oil over, and sprinkle with a pinch of fleur de sel. Place 1 avocado half over, drizzle them all with a little more lemon juice, olive oil, and salt. Place a few slices of onion over each half, and sprinkle with pepper.

1 recipe Green Goddess Dressing (see page 208)

12 strips (10 ounces) thick-cut bacon, preferably applewood-smoked (optional)

2 ripe avocados, cut in half lengthwise, pit removed and peeled

½ sweet spring onion, Maui, Vidalia, or Walla Walla, peeled and cut in half through the root end

4 slices white or whole-wheat sourdough bread (or see page 219)

1 garlic clove, peeled

1 bunch watercress, thick stems trimmed

2 tablespoons fresh lemon juice

Extra-virgin olive oil, for drizzling over the sandwiches

Fleur de sel or kosher salt, to taste

Freshly cracked black pepper, to taste

GOAT CHEESE AND FENNEL ON WALNUT TOAST

Several years ago, an old friend and I crossed paths in Paris. Knowing we had a lot to catch up on, I chose a quiet, low-key restaurant: L'Assiette. Stilted and a little awkward, our conversation didn't really get going until the food arrived at our table. It turned out to be one of the most memorable meals I had ever eaten, as well as one of the most inspirational dishes for this book.

My first course was a mesclun salad flanked by a tartine made of thick, hand-cut slices of toasted country bread crowned with 3 white discs of Crottin de Chavignol goat cheese, each sprinkled with a different herb or spice. As I picked at the greens with one hand and ate the goat-cheese tartine with the other, our dialogue finally began to pick up speed, taking on the rhythm of the meal. Every time I make this sandwich, I think of my friend Kerry Caloyannidis and that wonderful evening in Paris. I knew that someday I would find room on one of my menus to re-create this simple, soulful dish.

The addition of stewed fennel makes this a meal, instead of a first course. If you're only going to use one type of goat cheese, choose one that is full-flavored, like the one I ate in Paris. But if you want more variety in flavor and shape, use three different types of goat cheese: a small wedge of aged goat cheese, a half-moon of creamy, fresh goat cheese, and a triangle of washed-rind goat cheese. They probably won't soften at the same temperatures, so heat the firmer cheese first and then add the others.

Preheat the oven to 450 degrees.

TO PREPARE THE FENNEL: Slice the fennel into ¼-inch-thick slices and cut them into ¼-inch-squares.

In a medium skillet, over medium-high heat, toast the fennel seeds for 2–3 minutes, until they begin to release their aroma. Transfer to a bowl.

In the same skillet, warm the olive oil over medium heat. Add the fennel and onion, and cook for about 10 minutes, until just tender. Stir in the Pernod, fennel seeds, salt, and pepper, and cook for another minute. Remove from the heat. Season with salt, cracked black pepper, and Pernod, to taste.

FOR THE FENNEL

1 fennel bulb, outer stalks removed and discarded, fronds reserved

1 tablespoon fennel seeds

¼ cup extra-virgin olive oil

½ medium red onion, peeled and chopped into ¼-inch squares

1 tablespoon Pernod

1 teaspoon kosher salt

Freshly cracked black pepper, to taste

4 slices walnut, white, or whole-wheat sourdough bread (or see page 219)

1 garlic clove, peeled

FOR THE GOAT CHEESE

8 ounces total of 3 different types of goat cheese, sliced into ¼-inch-thick wedges or discs or triangles

Extra-virgin olive oil, for drizzling

⅛ teaspoon cayenne pepper

¼ teaspoon freshly cracked black pepper

Pinch of fresh thyme leaves

16 small sprigs fennel frond

Grill the bread according to the directions on page 8. Rub one side of each slice of bread with the garlic, and place on a baking sheet, garlic side up. TO ASSEMBLE THE SANDWICHES: Spoon about 3 tablespoons of the fennel over each slice of bread. Place a wedge or disc of each type of goat cheese (for 3 total) spaced evenly over the fennel. Heat the sandwiches in the oven for about 3–4 minutes, until the cheese just begins to soften and melt (being careful not to brown the cheese). Drizzle them with a little olive oil, and sprinkle one of the cheeses with cayenne, another with pepper, and another with thyme leaves. Scatter 3 or 4 small fennel frond sprigs over the top of each.

BRAISED ARTICHOKES, RICOTTA, AND MINT PESTO WITH PINE-NUT CURRANT RELISH

Although my original rendition with artichokes, ricotta, and mint pesto was popular on Sandwich Night, I always felt that the sandwich wasn't quite right and that something was missing. The Sicilian agrodolce *combination of pine nuts, currants, and balsamic vinegar added that final note the sandwich was yearning for. Now, when I make this sandwich, I know it's just perfect.*

If you choose to purchase marinated artichokes instead of braising them yourself, look for Roman-style, long-stemmed ones sold in bulk and marinated in sunflower oil. Search for a locally made fresh ricotta cheese. Unlike the industrial supermarket version, fresh ricotta is soft, wet, and full-flavored and may not require quite as much olive oil to season and soften it.

FOR THE ARTICHOKES: Remove the tough outer leaves of the artichokes, and cut off the top third of each. Using a sharp knife, trim off the tough outer surface of the bottoms and stems of the artichokes.

FOR THE ARTICHOKES
4 medium or large artichokes, or
4 marinated Roman-style
artichoke hearts, cut into quarters
1½–2½ cups extra-virgin olive oil
1 lemon, cut in half
1 medium yellow onion, thinly sliced
1 whole dried red chile
4 garlic cloves, peeled
and thinly sliced
2 teaspoons kosher salt
1 4-inch sprig fresh rosemary

Pour the olive oil into a medium saucepan. Squeeze the juice of the lemon halves into the saucepan, and add the lemon halves, onion, chile, garlic, salt, rosemary sprig, and artichokes. Over medium heat, bring them to a boil. Turn down to a simmer, and cook about 10–15 minutes, until the artichokes are fork-tender. Allow to cool completely.

Remove the artichokes from the oil. Strain the oil, and discard the lemon, onion, garlic, chile, and rosemary. Reserve the oil to use in the ricotta spread and pesto.

Cut the artichokes in half and remove the fibrous choke. Cut each piece of artichoke in half again.

FOR THE PINE-NUT CURRANT RELISH: Adjust the oven rack to the middle position, and preheat the oven to 325 degrees. Spread the pine nuts on a baking sheet, and toast in the oven for about 8–10 minutes, until lightly browned.

In a very small saucepan, combine the currants and balsamic vinegar, and cook over low heat about 3–4 minutes, until the currants are softened and plump. Remove from the heat and set aside.

Heat about 2 tablespoons of the artichoke olive oil (or, if the artichokes haven't finished cooking yet, use 2 tablespoons extra-virgin olive oil) in a small sauté pan or skillet. Cook the onion, garlic, chile, salt, and rosemary about 5 minutes, until the onion is translucent. Remove from the heat, combine with the currant mixture and add the pine nuts. Allow to cool.

FOR THE RICOTTA SPREAD: In a medium bowl, combine the ricotta, olive oil, and salt, to taste.

Grill the bread according to the directions on page 8. Rub one side of each slice of bread with the garlic clove, and place garlic side up.

TO ASSEMBLE THE SANDWICHES: Spread an uneven layer of the ricotta mixture over each slice of bread, and spoon a couple of teaspoons of pesto over it. Cut each slice in half on the diagonal, and place on the serving plates.

Arrange the artichoke quarters facing in opposite directions over each half-slice of bread, and fan out slightly. Spoon a tablespoon of the currant–pine-nut mixture over each half, and shave 3 or 4 thin slices of cheese over them. Drizzle some of the remaining olive oil over the tops of the sandwiches.

FOR THE PINE-NUT
CURRANT RELISH
2 tablespoons pine nuts
Just under ½ cup currants
¼ cup balsamic vinegar
3 tablespoons finely chopped
red onion
¼ teaspoon finely chopped garlic
1 whole dried red chile
¼ teaspoon kosher salt, or to taste
½ sprig fresh rosemary

FOR THE RICOTTA
1¼ cups (¾ pound) fresh
ricotta cheese
Approximately ¼ cup plus 3 tablespoons extra-virgin olive oil (from
the braised artichokes)
1 teaspoon kosher salt

4 slices white or whole-wheat sourdough bread (or see page 219)
1 garlic clove, peeled

1 recipe Mint Pesto (see page 212),
using the oil from the artichokes
to make the pesto
Approximately ¼-pound wedge
Parmigiano-Reggiano, for shaving
over the tops of the sandwiches

GRILLED ESCAROLE,
WHITE BEAN PURÉE,
AND BACON

I am certainly not the first person to combine pork, beans, and greens. But I'm pretty sure I've never seen Parmigiano-Reggiano added to any of those dishes. And certainly not all together on one sandwich!

FOR THE WHITE-BEAN PURÉE: In a medium saucepan, combine the beans, bacon, rosemary, sage leaves, bay leaf, garlic, 1 teaspoon of the balsamic vinegar, salt, and pepper in about 2½ cups water, and bring to a boil over medium-high heat. Turn the heat to medium-low, and simmer for about 2 hours, until the beans are soft and tender. Check frequently, adding water as necessary to keep the beans immersed in water.

Strain the beans, reserving the liquid. Return the liquid to the saucepan, and reduce it over high heat until you have about 1 cup of slightly thickened and opaque liquid.

Remove the herbs from the beans and discard. Remove the garlic, squeeze out the soft pulp from the cloves into the beans, and discard the garlic head and peels. Remove the bacon, cut it into small pieces, and set aside.

In a food mill set over a bowl, or a food processor fitted with a metal blade, process the beans until they form a coarse purée. Add the bacon back to the beans, and pour in the reduced liquid, remaining balsamic vinegar, and olive oil, stirring to combine. Season with salt, pepper, and balsamic vinegar, to taste.

FOR THE ESCAROLE: Toss the escarole with 2 tablespoons of the olive oil, 1 teaspoon of the salt, and a few grindings of pepper. Let stand for 5 minutes.

Over a hot grill, char the escarole 7–8 minutes on each side, until tender. Alternatively, to char on the stovetop: Heat a heavy-duty skillet over high

FOR THE WHITE BEAN PURÉE

1 cup dried beans, such as cannelini, flageolet, Great Northern, or French navy

1 2-ounce piece of bacon, preferably applewood-smoked

1 3-inch sprig fresh rosemary

3 fresh sage leaves

1 bay leaf

1 head garlic, cut in half crosswise, reserving one half for another use

1 tablespoon balsamic vinegar

1 teaspoon kosher salt

Freshly cracked black pepper, to taste

¼ cup plus 1 tablespoon extra-virgin olive oil

FOR THE ESCAROLE

1 medium head escarole, cut in half lengthwise

¼ cup plus 2 tablespoons extra-virgin olive oil

1½ teaspoons kosher salt

Freshly cracked black pepper, to taste

1 tablespoon plus 1 teaspoon red-wine vinegar

1–2 garlic cloves, peeled and finely chopped (about 1½ teaspoons)

heat. Add the escarole, and char on one side for 7–8 minutes. Turn over and char the other side. Remove from the skillet. In either case, discard any pieces that are too blackened. Allow to cool. Cut off the root and discard it, then chop the escarole coarsely into 1-inch pieces.

In a large bowl, whisk together the vinegar, garlic, remaining oil and salt, and pepper to taste. Add the escarole, and allow it to marinate for at least 15–30 minutes before serving.

FOR THE BACON: In a small skillet, over medium heat, cook the bacon until cooked all the way through but not crisp. Drain on a paper towel.

Grill the bread according to the directions on page 8. Rub one side of each slice of bread with the garlic clove, and cut each slice in half on the diagonal. Place the slices on serving plates, garlic side up.

TO ASSEMBLE THE SANDWICHES: Pile an uneven layer of escarole over each half-slice, and scatter the bacon over it. Spoon the bean purée onto the center, leaving a 1-inch border of escarole, and top with 3 or 4 shavings of cheese. Drizzle with olive oil.

2 ¼-inch-thick strips bacon, preferably applewood-smoked, cut diagonally into ¼-inch-thick pieces

4 slices white or whole-wheat sourdough bread (or see page 219)
1 garlic clove, peeled
Approximately ¼-pound wedge
Parmigiano-Reggiano, for shaving
over the tops of the sandwiches
Extra-virgin olive oil, for drizzling
on the sandwiches

BRANDADE, ROASTED TOMATOES, AND CHICKPEAS

In France, salted dried cod is reconstituted and made into brandade, the classic dish of the southern region. Our chef at Campanile, Chris Kidder, makes his brandade completely from scratch. Instead of buying the cod already preserved, he starts the process with fresh halibut or cod, salting it and letting it dehydrate for a week. Cooked in milk with garlic and potatoes, the fish transforms into a tasty, rich purée, delicious on its own or as a sandwich with roasted tomatoes and chickpeas.

If you want to make the brandade from scratch, start a week ahead of time with a fresh piece of halibut or cod, and just follow the recipe. If you buy commercial baccalà that's already salted and dried (available at most Greek, Spanish, or Italian delis), start the recipe at the point where the fish gets soaked in water for 24 hours to remove most of the salt. Be sure to taste your brandade after it's puréed; even though you've gone to the trouble of removing the salt, you may need to add more at the end.

All of the components of this sandwich can be made a couple of days in advance and stored in the refrigerator. The chickpeas are so delicious that I suggest you double the recipe and use the other half in salads and soups. The chickpea broth is also so tasty you'll want to save it for soup stock.

TO SALT THE FISH: Place the fish on a non-corrosive, stainless-steel perforated pan (or steamer basket or colander) set on a baking sheet. Pour a third of the salt over the fish, flip it over, and pour another third of the salt over that side. Flip the fish over again, and pour the remaining salt over it. The fillet should be completely covered in salt. Cover the pan and baking sheet tightly with plastic wrap, and refrigerate 5–7 days, until the fish is firm and stiff. As the salt leaches the moisture out of the fish, you'll need to empty the liquid that collects underneath it every few days.

Rinse off the fillet, transfer it to a deep bowl, and cover it with at least 4 inches of water. Cover the bowl with plastic wrap, and store in the refriger-

FOR THE SALTED FISH
6 ounces halibut or cod fillet, ½ inch to 1 inch thick, or 4 ounces store-bought dried salt cod or baccalà
Approximately 2 cups kosher salt, if using fresh fish

FOR THE CHICKPEAS
¾ cup dried chickpeas
1 bay leaf
4 sprigs fresh thyme
1 teaspoon kosher salt
¼ teaspoon freshly cracked black pepper
1–1½ cups extra-virgin olive oil
1 whole dried red chile

FOR THE TOMATOES
32 Sweet 100's, or 16 halved small red cherry tomatoes
1 teaspoon finely chopped fresh thyme leaves
½ teaspoon finely chopped fresh rosemary

FOR THE BRANDADE
1–2 cups whole milk (depending on size of pan)
10 garlic cloves, peeled

ator overnight or for about 8–10 hours. Change the water in the morning and continue soaking the rest of the day, or for another 8–10 hours. (To remove most of the salt, the fish must soak at least 24 hours, but no longer than 36 hours.) Rinse and drain the fish, wrap in plastic, and refrigerate until ready to use.

TO PREPARE THE CHICKPEAS: Place the dried chickpeas in a bowl with water to cover, and soak overnight. Drain the chickpeas and place them in a small saucepan with water to cover. Add the bay leaf, 2 sprigs of the thyme, salt, and pepper, and bring to a boil over high heat. Turn the heat down to medium low, and simmer 1–2 hours, until tender, adding water as necessary to keep the chickpeas immersed in water. Taste a chickpea to make sure it's cooked all the way through.

Drain the chickpeas (saving the liquid for another use), and transfer back to the pot. Add at least a cup of the olive oil (enough to cover the chickpeas), the remaining thyme, and the chile, and simmer over low heat for about 30 minutes, until the chickpeas absorb some of the olive oil and are creamy in texture and slightly darkened in color. Allow them to cool in the olive oil. Strain, and use the olive oil to make the tomatoes and brandade.

TO ROAST THE TOMATOES: Adjust the oven rack to the middle position, and preheat the oven to 400 degrees.

Toss the tomatoes with 2 tablespoons of the olive oil from the chickpeas, and the herbs. Transfer to a baking sheet, and roast for about 10 minutes, until the tomatoes begin to release their juices and the skins begin to wrinkle. Remove them from the oven and allow to cool.

TO PREPARE THE BRANDADE: Cut the fish into 3 chunks, and place in a medium saucepan. Pour the milk over to cover, add the garlic cloves and potato, and bring to a low boil. Turn down to a simmer, and cook for 15–20 minutes, until the potato is fork-tender and cooked all the way through. Strain and discard the milk.

In the same saucepan, bring the cream to a boil, and turn off the heat immediately. Place the fish, potato, and garlic in the bowl of an electric mixer and, using the paddle attachment, mix on low for about 1 minute, until the ingredients are incorporated. Alternatively, mash the ingredients together by hand with a potato masher or whisk. Add enough cream so that the mixture

1 medium white potato, peeled and
cut into 8 1-inch chunks
½–¾ cup heavy cream
2–4 tablespoons extra-virgin olive oil
(from the chickpeas,
if already prepared)
½ teaspoon kosher salt
Freshly cracked white pepper, to taste

4 slices white or whole-wheat sourdough bread (or see page 219)
1 garlic clove, peeled
Approximately 20 fresh Italian
parsley leaves

is the consistency of thick mashed potatoes. Add the olive oil (from the chickpeas, if you have made them already), and mix about 1 more minute. Season with salt and white pepper, to taste.

Grill the bread according to the directions on page 8. Rub one side of each slice of bread with the garlic clove, and place on serving plates, garlic side up.

TO ASSEMBLE THE SANDWICHES: Spread an uneven layer of brandade over the bread, and spoon the chickpeas over it. Scatter the tomatoes and parsley leaves over the sandwiches, and drizzle them with a little of the leftover olive oil.

BRANDADE, SAUTÉED PEA TENDRILS, POACHED EGG, AND MOROCCAN OLIVES

The classic Provençal combination of eggs and salt cod gets an exotic twist here with fresh pea tendrils and Moroccan olives. Asking me which brandade sandwich I like better—the chickpea-with-roasted-tomato version or this one—is like asking me to choose my favorite child. Impossible! You, however, can make your choice after trying both of them. If you're making Brandade from scratch (page 50), you'll need to begin the process a week in advance. If you're using store-bought salt cod, you'll need to begin 2 days ahead.

1 recipe Brandade
(see page 50)

FOR THE OLIVES
20 Moroccan oil-cured olives, pitted
¼ cup extra-virgin olive oil

FOR THE PEA TENDRILS
¼ cup extra-virgin olive oil
Approximately 4 cups pea tendrils,
loosely packed (about 4–5 ounces),
or 8 cups baby-spinach or arugula
leaves, loosely packed
(about 4–5 ounces)
1 teaspoon finely chopped shallot
1 garlic clove, peeled and finely
chopped (1 teaspoon)

4 slices white or whole-wheat sourdough bread (or see page 219)
1 garlic clove, peeled

FOR THE EGGS
2 tablespoons white-wine vinegar
Pinch of kosher salt
4 extra-large eggs

Approximately 20 fresh Italian
parsley leaves

In a small saucepan, over medium-low heat, warm the olives in the olive oil for a few minutes. Strain the olives, reserving the oil. Allow them to cool and tear in half.

TO MAKE THE PEA TENDRILS: In a large sauté pan, over medium-high heat, warm the olive oil a minute or two. Add the pea tendrils (or greens), and cook a minute, just to wilt. Add the shallot and garlic, and cook for another minute, until softened but not colored, stirring frequently.

Grill the bread according to the directions on page 8. Rub one side of each slice of bread with the garlic clove, and place on serving plates, garlic side up. Pile the pea tendrils (or greens) unevenly on the bread, allowing them to drape over the edges slightly. In a small saucepan over low heat, warm the brandade. Spoon the brandade over the pea tendrils, leaving a 1-inch border of greens around the edge.

TO POACH THE EGGS: In a medium saucepan, bring 2 quarts of water to a boil. Turn the heat down to just below a simmer, and add the vinegar and salt. Crack an egg into a small bowl to check that the yolk isn't broken. Slowly stir the water in one direction to create a whirlpool effect. Once the

whirlpool has slowed down a little, carefully slide the egg into the water against the side of the pan, following the current of the water as you pour the egg in, so that the white envelops the yolk. Crack another egg into the small bowl, and add to the water in the same manner. Poach the eggs for 2 to 2½ minutes, until the whites are set and the yolks are runny. Carefully remove with a slotted spoon to a plate to drain. Cupping the eggs in your hand, tip the plate to pour off the excess water. Place the eggs over the center of the greens. Prepare the other 2 eggs in the same manner.

(If you want to prepare the eggs ahead of time, slip the poached eggs into a bowl of ice water, and just before assembling the sandwiches, return them to the simmering water for 10–20 seconds to warm.)

Scatter the olives and parsley leaves over the top, and drizzle over the sandwiches some of the oil in which the olives were warmed.

Piled-High Pork Sandwich

This is the sandwich to make in the fall, when you stop eating steamed vegetables and put away your skimpy bathing suit. One bite of this roast-pork-loin sandwich with yams, bitter greens, and brown butter, and you'll be glad that summer is finally over.

For a super flavorful and tender pork loin, brine the meat a full 2 days. To pile the pork as high as I do, you have to shave it super-thin. Hone your slicing skills, buy a meat slicer, or make friends with someone who has one. If you don't, your sandwich will still be as delicious as mine, it just won't be piled quite as high.

TO MAKE THE BRINE: In a small non-reactive pot, combine 2 cups of the water, the salt, sugar, bay leaves, thyme, allspice, fennel seeds, juniper berries, cloves, and rosemary branches. Bring the mixture to a boil over high heat, and immediately remove it from the heat. Add about 5 more cups of water, and allow it to cool to room temperature. Refrigerate the brine until it's well chilled, at least 2 hours.

Place the pork in the brine. It should be completely immersed in liquid; if not, add a little more water. Cover the bowl tightly with plastic wrap, and marinate the pork for 2 full days (no longer) in the refrigerator.

Preheat the oven to 350 degrees.

TO COOK THE PORK LOIN: Cut 3 12-inch-long pieces of kitchen twine. Position the pork flesh side up (or fat side down), and, starting about an inch from one end, wrap a piece of twine once around the meat and tie it in a tight knot on the top surface of the loin. Continue with the rest of the loin, spacing the ties about an inch apart.

Mound the onion slices in the center of a small baking dish (just large enough to hold the pork). Place the pork, flesh side down, on top of the onions, and drizzle both the pork and the onions with the olive oil. Roast in the oven for about 1 hour, until the meat reaches an internal temperature of 140 degrees on a meat thermometer. Remove from the oven, and allow to cool completely.

FOR THE BRINE
Approximately 6–8 cups water
½ cup plus 2 tablespoons kosher salt
⅓ cup sugar
2 bay leaves
1 tablespoon dried thyme
1 teaspoon cracked whole allspice
1 teaspoon fennel seeds
½ teaspoon crushed juniper berries
3 whole cloves
2 branches fresh rosemary
1½ pounds pork loin

FOR ROASTING THE PORK
1 large yellow onion, peeled and thinly sliced
¼ cup extra-virgin olive oil

FOR THE YAM PURÉE
1–2 large jewel or garnet yams (1½ pounds)
1 stick (4 ounces) unsalted butter
1 small bunch fresh sage
2 whole cloves
½ cinnamon stick
Kosher salt, to taste
Freshly cracked black pepper, to taste

FOR THE BALSAMIC-SAGE BROWN BUTTER
1 stick (4 ounces) unsalted butter
8 whole fresh sage leaves

Using a very sharp knife or meat slicer, slice the pork into paper-thin slices by carefully sawing back and forth through the meat.

Remove any blackened onions from the baking dish (to eat or discard), and transfer the remaining cooked onions to a small sauté pan. If they seem dry, drizzle over a little olive oil. Sauté the onions over low heat until they are very soft and caramelized, about 15 minutes.

FOR THE PURÉED YAMS: While the pork is cooking, put the yam in the oven with it. Bake the yam for 1 to 1½ hours, until soft in the center. Allow to cool, and remove the skin. In a small skillet or sauté pan, melt the butter with the bunch of sage over medium-high heat. After a few minutes, the butter will become foamy and begin to darken. Swirl the pan to promote the even browning of the butter, taking care that it doesn't burn. When it begins to bubble somewhat vigorously, add the cloves and cinnamon stick. Continue cooking a few more minutes, until the bubbles subside and the liquid is dark brown and has a nutty, toasty aroma.

Using a fine-mesh strainer or a food mill placed over a bowl, purée the yams until they have a smooth consistency. Using a fine-mesh sieve, strain the browned-butter mixture into the yams. Whisk them together to incorporate, and season with salt and pepper, to taste.

TO MAKE THE BALSAMIC-SAGE BROWN BUTTER: In a small skillet or saucepan, heat the butter, sage leaves, and salt over medium heat. Brown the butter in the same manner as for the puréed yams, above. Stir in the balsamic vinegar and season with vinegar and salt, to taste.

Grill the bread according to the directions on page 8. Rub one side of each slice of bread with the garlic clove. Cut each slice in half on the diagonal and place on serving plates, garlic side up.

TO ASSEMBLE THE SANDWICHES: Arrange the caramelized onions and an uneven layer of the greens on each half-slice. Spoon the yam purée over, leaving a 1-inch border of greens around the edge. Pile the pork, sprinkling it with fleur de sel and drizzling some of the balsamic-sage brown butter as you layer the meat. Continue piling the pork until it's about 1½ inches high. Scatter the sage leaves over the sandwiches.

1 teaspoon kosher salt
1 tablespoon plus 1 teaspoon
balsamic vinegar

1 recipe Sautéed Bitter Greens
(see page 32)
4 slices white or whole-wheat
sourdough bread (or see page 219)
1 garlic clove, peeled
Fleur de sel, to taste

SAUTÉED CHICKEN LIVERS, BRAISED CELERY, AND BACON BREADCRUMBS

When I invite you over for a chicken-liver sandwich, don't be so quick to turn your nose up. My version, with bacon breadcrumbs and braised celery, happens to be just delicious.

TO PREPARE THE CELERY: Adjust the oven rack to the middle position, and preheat the oven to 450 degrees.

Cut the celery vertically in half through the root, and wash thoroughly to remove all sand and grit, being careful not to break apart the hearts. Shake to remove the excess water. Remove about 20 pale leaves to use for the bacon breadcrumbs and garnish.

Arrange the celery, cut side up, in a 9-by-13-inch baking dish (it is important that the celery fits snugly). Pour in the chicken stock and oil, and sprinkle with the thyme, salt, and pepper. Cover the dish tightly with plastic wrap, then aluminum foil, and braise in the oven for about 50 minutes.

Remove the foil, puncture the plastic to allow the steam to escape, then remove the plastic. Return the celery to the oven, and cook, uncovered, for 45 more minutes, until it's tender and caramelized. Allow to cool, and reserve the liquid. (You should have about $\frac{1}{2}$ cup of liquid.) Cut the root ends off the celery and discard, then cut the celery in half horizontally.

TO PREPARE THE BACON BREADCRUMBS: Turn the oven down to 325 degrees.

Brush one side of the 1–2 slices of bread with oil, and place, oil side up, on a baking sheet. Toast in the oven for about 10–15 minutes, until lightly browned. Rub the bread with the garlic clove, and allow to cool. In a food processor fitted with a metal blade, or by hand, grind or chop the bread until finely ground. It should measure about $\frac{1}{2}$ cup.

In a very large skillet (large enough to hold all of the livers) over medium heat, cook the bacon until cooked all the way through but not crisp. Remove

FOR THE BRAISED CELERY

1 head celery,
large outer stalks removed
1½ cups chicken stock, homemade
or store-bought low-sodium variety
2 tablespoons extra-virgin olive oil
12 3-inch sprigs fresh thyme
½ teaspoon kosher salt
¼ teaspoon freshly cracked
black pepper

FOR THE BACON BREADCRUMBS

1–2 slices white or whole-wheat
sourdough bread (or see page 219)
1 tablespoon extra-virgin olive oil
1 garlic clove, peeled
2 strips (2 ounces) thick-cut bacon,
preferably applewood-smoked
1 scallion, dark-green stems removed
and discarded, finely chopped
1 tablespoon finely chopped
fresh chives
1 tablespoon finely chopped
celery leaves (from above)
½ teaspoon finely chopped
lemon zest
1 tablespoon finely chopped
fresh Italian parsley leaves

the bacon, and drain on paper towels, reserving the bacon fat in the skillet. Finely chop the bacon.

In a large bowl, toss to combine the breadcrumbs, bacon, scallion, chives, celery leaves, lemon zest, parsley, and pepper.

Grill the bread according to the directions on page 8. Rub one side of each slice of bread with the garlic clove, and place on serving plates, garlic side up.

Arrange the celery over each slice of bread.

TO SAUTÉ THE CHICKEN LIVERS: Warm the reserved bacon fat and vegetable oil over high heat, until hot but not smoking. Sprinkle the livers with salt, and cook them for about 1–2 minutes on each side, until browned but still pink in the center. Add the brandy and stir, to deglaze the pan and coat the livers. Add the liquid from the celery and the chicken stock, and reduce for 2–3 minutes, until the mixture is thickened. Arrange the chicken livers over the celery, and spoon a tablespoon of the cooking liquid over each sandwich.

TO POACH THE EGGS: In a medium saucepan, bring 2 quarts of water to a boil. Turn the heat down to just below a simmer, and add the vinegar and kosher salt. Crack an egg into a small bowl to check that the yolk isn't broken. Slowly stir the water in one direction to create a whirlpool effect. Once the whirlpool has slowed down a little, carefully slide the egg into the water against the side of the pan, following the current of the water as you pour the egg in, so that the white envelops the yolk. Crack another egg into the small bowl, and add to the water in the same manner. Poach the eggs for 2 to 2½ minutes, until the whites are set and the yolks are runny. Carefully remove with a slotted spoon to a plate to drain. Cupping the eggs in your hand, tip the plate to pour off the excess water. Center the eggs over the livers. Prepare the other 2 eggs in the same manner.

(If you want to prepare the eggs ahead of time, slip the poached eggs into a bowl of ice water, and just before assembling the sandwiches, return them to the simmering water for 10–20 seconds to warm.)

Using a knife, slash the poached eggs through the center to allow the yolks to run. Sprinkle the eggs with a little fleur de sel. Sprinkle over the breadcrumbs and scatter a few celery leaves on top.

½ teaspoon freshly cracked black pepper
4 slices white or whole-wheat sourdough bread (or see page 219)
1 garlic clove, peeled

FOR THE CHICKEN LIVERS
2–3 tablespoons vegetable oil
12 chicken livers, rinsed and dried
2 teaspoons kosher salt
¼ cup brandy or cognac
½ cup chicken stock

FOR THE EGGS
4 extra-large eggs
2 tablespoons white-wine vinegar
Pinch of kosher salt
Fleur de sel, to taste

PORTOBELLO MUSHROOMS, BRAISED ENDIVE, AND TELEME CHEESE

Portobellos are the steak of the vegetable world. When roasted or grilled, these overgrown, meaty, substantial mushrooms turn into something you can really sink your teeth into. Look for large portobellos, with caps roughly 6 inches in diameter. Once they are sliced and slightly overlapped on the bread, two of these oversized mushrooms will be enough for each sandwich.

Teleme, a mild domestic cow's-milk cheese made by the Peluso family in Los Banos, California, not only adds a smooth white finish when melted over the top of the sandwich, but also acts as the flavor counterpoint to the earthy mushrooms and rich braised endive. If you can't find Teleme, an Italian Stracchino or Bellwether Farms Crescenza is a good substitute.

Adjust the oven rack to the middle position, and preheat the oven to 400 degrees.

Arrange the endives in an ovenproof skillet or baking dish just large enough to hold them (it is important that the endives fit snugly). Add the olive oil, salt, pepper, chicken stock, cream, and tarragon stems. Cover tightly with plastic wrap and then foil, and bake for 35 minutes.

Remove the foil, puncture the plastic to allow the steam to escape, and then remove the plastic. Return the endives to the oven for 1 hour, until they're lightly browned and caramelized.

FOR THE MUSHROOMS: Place the mushrooms, stem side down, in 1 or 2 baking dishes just large enough to hold them. Pour the oil and vinegar over, and scatter the rosemary over them. Cover tightly with plastic wrap and then foil, and bake for 40 minutes.

Remove the foil, puncture the plastic to allow the steam to escape, and then remove the plastic. Return the mushrooms to the oven for 35–40 minutes, until the liquid is reduced and the mushrooms are nicely browned and

FOR THE ENDIVE

4 Belgian endives (about 6 ounces each), cut in half lengthwise

1 tablespoon extra-virgin olive oil

1 teaspoon kosher salt

¼ teaspoon freshly cracked black pepper

¾ cup chicken stock, homemade or the store-bought low-sodium variety

½ cup heavy cream

1–2 branches fresh tarragon, leaves removed and set aside for garnishing

FOR THE MUSHROOMS

8 large portobello mushrooms (about 6–8 ounces each)

3 tablespoons extra-virgin olive oil

3 tablespoons balsamic vinegar

1 3-inch branch fresh rosemary, sprigs removed from branch

4 slices white or whole-wheat sourdough bread (or see page 219)

1 garlic clove, peeled

8 ounces Teleme cheese

Extra-virgin olive oil, for drizzling on the sandwiches

tender. Allow them to cool, then slice each mushroom into ¼-inch-thick slices.

Adjust the oven rack to the upper position, and preheat the broiler.

Grill the bread according to the directions on page 8. Rub one side of each slice of bread with the garlic clove, and place the slices on a baking sheet, garlic side up.

TO ASSEMBLE THE SANDWICHES: Place 2 whole sliced mushrooms over each slice of bread, fanning them out slightly to cover the bread. Place two endive halves, cut side up, to cover the mushroom. Scatter a few small chunks of the cheese unevenly over the endive. Place the sandwiches under the broiler for about 1 minute, until the cheese is melted. Drizzle the mushrooms with a little olive oil, and sprinkle with the reserved tarragon leaves, about 6–8 leaves per sandwich.

SAUTÉED BITTER GREENS WITH BEANS AND BACON (TWO WAYS)

There are two variations on this sandwich. Both call for sautéed bitter greens and beans and bacon. In the winter version, dried white beans and bacon are braised overnight in the oven. Before you go to bed, put them in the oven; set your alarm, and don't oversleep. In the springtime or summer, make a lighter version with fresh fava beans or fresh lima beans that are first stewed in olive oil and then puréed and topped with strands of cooling mint.

Whether you choose to make this sandwich in the winter or in the spring, its hearty, rich flavors are always comforting.

TO PREPARE THE BRAISED BACON: Adjust the oven rack to the middle position, and preheat the oven to 200 degrees.

FOR THE BRAISED BACON
1 8-ounce slab of bacon, preferably applewood-smoked, cut into 4 2-by-3-inch pieces
2 teaspoons vegetable oil
½ medium onion, finely chopped
½ carrot, peeled and finely chopped
½ celery stalk, finely chopped
½ cup white wine
2 tablespoons wildflower honey
½ cup chicken stock, homemade or the store-bought low-sodium variety

In a small saucepan, bring 1 cup of water to a boil, turn down to a simmer, and poach the bacon for 5 minutes. Drain the bacon, reserving the liquid.

In a 1½-quart ovenproof saucepan, over medium-high heat, combine the oil, onion, carrot, and celery, and cook for 5 minutes, until lightly browned. Add the wine, and reduce until the liquid is almost completely evaporated. Add the honey, and cook for about 5 minutes over medium-low heat. Add the chicken stock, bring the mixture to a boil, and remove from the heat. Add the bacon, and cover the saucepan tightly with plastic wrap and then foil. Braise in the oven for 8–10 hours or overnight. Remove the foil, puncture the plastic to allow the steam to escape, and then remove the plastic. Cool and refrigerate, and rewarm when ready to use.

TO PREPARE THE DRIED BEANS: In a 2–3-quart saucepan, combine the beans, onion, thyme, carrot, celery, chile, oil, salt, and garlic. Measure the bacon poaching liquid, adding water until it equals 2 cups total, and pour it into the saucepan. Cover the pan tightly with plastic wrap and foil, and braise in the oven for 8–10 hours, until the beans are tender and creamy and are beginning to fall apart. Remove the foil and plastic. Cool and refrigerate, and rewarm when ready to use.

TO MAKE THE FAVA OR LIMA PURÉE: Remove the favas or limas from their pods. In a medium saucepan, bring 4 cups of water and 2 table-spoons of salt to a boil. Cook the beans for 2 minutes in the boiling water. Drain them, and place in a large bowl of ice water to cool. Using your fingers, squeeze the beans to remove the outer skins, and discard the skins.

In the same saucepan, combine the beans, olive oil, and garlic. Over low heat, bring the beans to a simmer, and cook them for about 5 minutes, until tender. Over a bowl, strain and reserve the olive oil from the beans, and remove and discard the garlic.

In a food mill set over a bowl, or in a food processor fitted with a metal blade, briefly process the beans (being careful not to aerate them) until they form a coarse purée. By hand, stir in the oil from the beans so the purée is smooth without being runny. (If you have leftover olive oil, reserve it for drizzling over the sandwiches.) Season the purée with lemon juice and salt, to taste. Cool and refrigerate, and rewarm when ready to use.

FOR THE BRAISED
DRIED BEANS

1 cup dried small white beans, such as French navy or Tuscan

½ yellow onion, cut in half

2 3-inch sprigs fresh thyme

1 small carrot, peeled and cut into thirds

1 celery stalk, cut into thirds

1 whole dried red chile

1 cup extra-virgin olive oil

1 tablespoon kosher salt

3 garlic cloves, peeled

FOR THE FAVA BEANS

1 pound unshelled fresh fava or fresh lima beans (to equal about 2 cups shelled beans)

2 tablespoons plus 1 teaspoon kosher salt

¾ cup extra-virgin olive oil

1 garlic clove, peeled and cut in half

1–2 teaspoons fresh lemon juice, or to taste, plus more to squeeze over sandwiches

4 large fresh mint leaves

FOR THE SAUTÉED BACON

2 slices thick-cut bacon, preferably applewood-smoked, cut on the diagonal into ¼-inch-wide pieces

1 recipe Sautéed Bitter Greens (see page 32)

FOR THE BACON: In a small skillet over medium heat, cook the bacon until cooked all the way through but not crisp. Drain it on a paper towel.

Grill the bread according to the directions on page 8. Rub one side of each slice of bread with the garlic clove, and cut each slice in half on the diagonal. Place the slices on serving plates, garlic side up.

If you're making the fava-bean version, roll the mint leaves into tight cylinders and slice them into very thin slices. If you're making the braised bean version, cut each chunk of bacon into 4 pieces.

TO ASSEMBLE THE SANDWICHES: Pile an uneven layer of greens over each half-slice, and scatter the bacon over them. Spoon the beans over, leaving a 1-inch border of greens. Squeeze a few drops of lemon juice over them, and add a sprinkling of fleur de sel, to taste. (If you're making the fava- or lima-bean version, scatter the mint over them.) Shave 3 or 4 slices of cheese on each half, and drizzle olive oil over the top.

4 slices white or whole-wheat sourdough bread (or see page 219)
1 garlic clove, peeled
Fleur de sel or kosher salt, to taste
Approximately ¼-pound wedge Parmigiano-Reggiano, for shaving over the top of the sandwiches
Extra-virgin olive oil, for drizzling over the sandwiches

Long-Cooked Greens, Poached Egg, and Fontina Cheese

Cooked until tender and succulent, these Southern-style long-cooked greens turned out to be the perfect partner for a poached egg and Fontina. If you're not a true Southerner, you can leave out the ham hock.

Place the ham hock in a small pot with water to cover. Add the bay leaf, peppercorns, and juniper berries, and bring to a boil. Turn the heat down, and simmer for 2–3 hours, adding water as necessary to keep the ham hock immersed in water. Cook the ham hock until the meat falls away from the bone and the outer rind is completely tender and softened.

Remove the ham hock from the liquid, and allow it to cool. Over high heat, reduce the liquid by half, until it's thickened and gelatinous. Remove from the heat, and discard the juniper berries and bay leaf.

TO PREPARE THE GREENS: While the ham hock is cooking, in a large pot, bring 8 cups of water and ¼ cup of the salt to a boil. Remove the stems and center ribs of the greens and slice them on the diagonal into 1-inch-thick pieces. Cook the greens and stems and ribs in the boiling water (in 2 or 3 batches) for about 2 minutes, until wilted. Drain, and place in a large bowl of ice water to chill. Drain well, and squeeze out excess water.

In a large skillet, over medium heat, sauté the onion, garlic, stems, ribs, chile, and remaining 2 teaspoons of salt in the olive oil for 3–4 minutes, until softened. Add the greens, turn the heat down to low, and cook about 1 hour or more, until tender. Discard the chile.

Using your fingers, pick the meat and fat off of the ham hock and chop it into small pieces. Discard the bone. Add the reduced liquid (you should have about 1 cup) and chopped meat to the greens, stirring to incorporate. Over medium-low heat, cook another 30 minutes, until the greens are very soft and tender. Season with salt and pepper, to taste.

FOR THE HAM HOCK
(OPTIONAL)
1 ham hock
1 bay leaf
4 peppercorns
4 juniper berries

FOR THE GREENS
¼ cup plus 2 teaspoons kosher salt
2–3 bunches (about 1¼ pounds) Swiss chard, kale, escarole, collard greens or a combination of them
1 small onion, sliced into ¼-inch-thick slices
8 garlic cloves, peeled and thinly sliced
1 whole dried red chile
½ cup extra-virgin olive oil
Freshly cracked black pepper, to taste
4 slices white or whole-wheat sourdough bread (or see page 219)
1 garlic clove, peeled

FOR THE EGGS
2 tablespoons white-wine vinegar
Pinch of kosher salt
4 extra-large eggs

3 ounces Fontina Val d'Aosta or Gruyère cheese, sliced into 4 ⅛-inch-thick slices

Adjust the oven rack to the upper position, and preheat the broiler.

Grill the bread according to the directions on page 8. Rub one side of each slice of bread with the garlic clove, and place the slices on a baking sheet, garlic side up. Pile the greens unevenly over the bread.

TO POACH THE EGGS: In a medium saucepan, bring 2 quarts of water to a boil. Turn the heat down to just below a simmer, and add the vinegar and salt. Crack an egg into a small bowl to check that the yolk isn't broken. Slowly stir the water in one direction to create a whirlpool effect. Once the whirlpool has slowed down a little, carefully slide the egg into the water against the side of the pan, following the current of the water as you pour the egg in, so that the white envelops the yolk. Crack another egg into the small bowl, and add to the water in the same manner. Poach the eggs for 2 to 2½ minutes, until the whites are set and the yolks are runny. Carefully remove with a slotted spoon to a plate to drain. Cupping the eggs in your hand, tip the plate to pour off the excess water. Place the eggs over the center of the greens. Prepare the other 2 eggs in the same manner.

(If you want to prepare the eggs ahead of time, slip the poached eggs into a bowl of ice water, and just before assembling the sandwiches, return the eggs to the simmering water for 10–20 seconds to warm.)

Drape a slice of Fontina cheese over each egg, and heat under the broiler for a minute or so, until the cheese is melted.

BEEF BRISKET HASH
ON TOAST

You may not want to eat the Clam Sandwich (see page 70) or Chopped "Sub" (see page 29) for breakfast, but this brisket-and-egg combo is satisfying any time of day. If you braise the beef all night long in the oven, your house will be filled with the rich, savory aromas of red wine, garlic, meat, and vegetables, and you may not be able to resist that craving for "hash and eggs" in the morning.

This recipe calls for a 3-pound piece of meat, which makes more than four sandwiches. Use the leftover brisket in a tomato sauce with pasta, or stuffed into a burrito. If you want to save yourself the trouble of making meat stock, look for a good-quality veal- or beef-stock concentrate, found in the frozen-food section at well-stocked supermarkets. This seemingly time-consuming recipe can be simplified by omitting the long-cooked greens.

In a large heavy-duty skillet, warm the oil over high heat. Add the carrot, fennel, onion, and celery, and cook for about 10 minutes, until the vegetables are very well browned.

In a small skillet, over medium-high heat, toast the mustard seeds, oregano, chiles, and bay leaves for 2–3 minutes, until the spices begin to release their aromas.

In a large bowl, combine the sautéed vegetables, toasted spices, tomato paste, garlic, thyme, and parsley. Add the red wine and beer.

Pat the meat dry with a paper towel. Rub the salt and pepper over the entire brisket, and place it in the bowl with the marinade. Cover it tightly with plastic wrap, and marinate in the refrigerator for 24 hours.

Adjust the oven rack to the middle position, and preheat the oven to 275 degrees.

FOR THE BRISKET: In a medium-sized heavy-duty Dutch oven (about the same length and width as the brisket) or a 4-quart saucepan, heat the oil over high heat until it's very hot and just begins to smoke. Remove the

FOR THE MARINADE

2 tablespoons vegetable oil

½ carrot, peeled and sliced
into 1-inch chunks

½ small fennel bulb, sliced
into 1-inch chunks

¼ onion, peeled and sliced
into 1-inch chunks

½ celery stalk, sliced
into 1-inch chunks

1 teaspoon yellow mustard seeds

1 teaspoon dried oregano

2 whole dried red chiles

2 bay leaves

1 tablespoon Italian tomato paste
(the kind that comes in a tube)

1 whole head garlic, unpeeled,
cut in half crosswise
and cut into chunks

1 sprig fresh thyme

1 sprig fresh Italian parsley

2½ cups red wine

¾ cup dark beer

1 3-pound brisket, preferably
the point cut

3 tablespoons kosher salt

3 tablespoons freshly cracked
black pepper

brisket from the marinade, scraping the vegetables off the meat and back into the marinade, reserving it to use later. Place the brisket in the pan, fat side down, and sear it until it's well browned, about 5 minutes on each side. Remove the meat, and transfer to a plate or cutting board.

Pour about ½ cup of the stock into the pan, and bring it to a boil over high heat, scraping the brown bits off the bottom of the pan. Remove the deglazed pan from the heat, and put the meat back in. Pour in the marinade and stock to cover about three-quarters of the meat. (Depending on the size of your pan, you may need to add more stock.) Cover the pan tightly with plastic wrap, then aluminum foil, and braise in the oven overnight or for 9 hours.

Remove the foil, puncture the plastic to allow the steam to escape, then remove the plastic. Allow the meat to cool in the liquid for about 45 minutes. TO ROAST THE CARROT: Turn the oven up to 500 degrees. Beginning at the wide end, cut the carrot into oblique slices by cutting off a ½-inch-thick slice at an angle, turning (or rolling) the carrot a half-turn, and slicing another piece off. Continue turning and slicing the carrot into pieces that resemble half-moon shapes. Toss the slices with the olive oil and salt, and transfer them to a baking dish. Roast them in the oven for about 20 minutes, until they're lightly browned and caramelized.

Transfer the meat (reserving the liquid) to a platter. Using a fine-mesh sieve, strain the brisket's braising liquid into a large bowl, pressing the vegetables against the strainer with a wooden spoon to extract their juices. Discard the vegetables and solids. Allow the liquid to cool another 10 minutes, then remove and discard the top layer of separated fat.

Transfer the braising liquid back to the roasting pan, and bring to a boil over high heat. Turn the heat down to medium, and cook for about 7 minutes, until the liquid is slightly thickened and reduced. Turn the heat to medium-low, whisk in the 3 tablespoons of butter, and cook for another minute or two, until the butter is melted and fully incorporated. Remove from the heat, and season with salt and pepper, to taste.

Using 2 forks, pull apart the meat, separating it into long, thin strands. Pour the reduced liquid over the meat, and stir in the roasted carrots.

1 recipe Long-Cooked Greens (optional, see page 65), without the ham hock and cooked a full 1½ hours, until very soft and tender

TO COOK THE BRISKET
2 tablespoons vegetable oil
2½ cups or more veal or beef stock, homemade or the store-bought low-sodium variety
3 tablespoons unsalted butter
Kosher salt, to taste
Freshly cracked black pepper, to taste

FOR THE CARROT
1 large carrot (about 12 ounces), peeled
2 teaspoons extra-virgin olive oil
2 tablespoons kosher salt

FOR THE HORSERADISH CREAM
¾ cup crème fraîche or sour cream
⅓ cup fresh horseradish purée (made in an electric juicer) or fresh horseradish from a deli
1 teaspoon kosher salt
Freshly cracked black pepper, to taste

4 slices white or whole-wheat sourdough bread (or see page 219)
1 garlic clove, peeled

FOR THE EGGS
2 tablespoons white-wine vinegar
Pinch of kosher salt
4 extra-large eggs

TO MAKE THE HORSERADISH CREAM: In a stainless-steel bowl, whisk together the crème fraîche and horseradish. Season with salt and pepper, to taste. Allow to sit at room temperature for at least 15 minutes to thicken slightly.

Grill the bread according to the directions on page 8. Rub one side of each slice of bread with the garlic clove, and place on serving plates, garlic side up.

TO ASSEMBLE THE SANDWICHES: If you're using the long-cooked greens, spoon them over the bread, and place about ½ cup of the brisket, a little of the liquid, and a few pieces of carrot over each slice of bread. Drizzle a tablespoon or so of the horseradish cream over.

TO POACH THE EGGS: In a medium saucepan, bring 2 quarts of water to a boil. Turn the heat down to just below a simmer, and add the vinegar and salt. Crack an egg into a small bowl. Slowly stir the water in one direction to create a whirlpool effect. Once the whirlpool has slowed down a little, carefully slide the egg into the water against the side of the pan, following the current of the water as you pour the egg in, so that the white envelops the yolk. Crack another egg into the small bowl, and add to the water in the same manner. Poach the eggs for 2 to 2½ minutes, until the whites are set and the yolks are runny. Carefully remove with a slotted spoon to a plate to drain. Cupping the eggs in your hand, tip the plate to pour off the excess water. Center a poached egg on top of each sandwich. Prepare the other 2 eggs in the same manner.

(If you want to prepare the eggs ahead of time, slip the poached eggs into a bowl of ice water, and just before assembling the sandwiches, return them to the simmering water for 10–20 seconds to warm.)

CLAM SANDWICH WITH PARMESAN BREADCRUMBS

Night after night, I used to lie awake dreaming of having my all-time favorite pizza. Since I didn't have a coal-fired pizza oven, and I lived in Los Angeles (too far away for delivery), I decided I'd have to re-create that New York clam pizza in the form of a sandwich. Clams sautéed in garlic butter and vermouth and piled on top of garlic toast almost satisfies my craving for a slice of Lombardi's clam pie.

TO FRY THE GARLIC: Place the garlic slices in a small saucepan with cold water to cover, and bring to a boil over medium heat. Drain the garlic, return it to the saucepan, and cover with cold water again. Bring to a boil, and remove from the heat. Drain well, and pat dry with a kitchen towel.

In the same small saucepan, over medium-high heat, warm the oil until just below a boil. Fry the garlic slices in the oil for a minute or two, stirring constantly and being careful not to burn them, until they're a pale-golden color. Remove immediately with a slotted spoon, and drain on paper towels. Reserve the oil for the clams.

FOR THE CLAMS: Soak the clams in cold water with the pepper for 30 minutes. Rinse well to remove any grit or sand.

TO MAKE THE GARLIC BUTTER: In a mortar and pestle, pulverize two-thirds of the garlic to a smooth paste. (If you don't have a mortar and pestle, finely chop the garlic and, using the back of a chef's knife, mash it into a paste.) In a small bowl, combine the garlic paste, remaining chopped garlic, butter, and parsley, and chill until ready to use.

TO MAKE THE BREADCRUMBS: Adjust the oven rack to the middle position, and preheat the oven to 325 degrees.

Brush one side of each slice of bread with olive oil, and place, oil side up, on a baking sheet. Toast in the oven for about 10–15 minutes, until firm and

FOR THE CRISP GARLIC
3 or 4 garlic cloves, each cut into about 20 paper-thin slices
¼ cup extra-virgin olive oil or vegetable oil

FOR THE CLAMS
50–60 Manila clams, or 32 littleneck clams, in the shell (about 4 pounds)
½ teaspoon freshly cracked black pepper
1 cup white vermouth
10 3-inch sprigs fresh thyme
2 whole dried red chiles

Approximately 1 tablespoon fresh lemon juice
Kosher salt, to taste

FOR THE GARLIC BUTTER
15 garlic cloves, peeled and finely chopped
2 sticks (8 ounces) unsalted butter, softened
1 tablespoon finely chopped fresh Italian parsley leaves

FOR THE BREADCRUMBS
1–2 slices white or whole-wheat sourdough bread (or see page 219)

lightly browned. Rub the bread with garlic and allow to cool. In a food processor fitted with a metal blade, or by hand, process or chop the bread until finely ground. You should have about $\frac{1}{4}$ cup.

In a small bowl, combine the breadcrumbs, Parmesan cheese, and parsley, and set aside.

TO COOK THE CLAMS: In a 12–14-inch skillet over high heat, heat 1 tablespoon of the garlic oil until very hot but not smoking. Add half of the clams, half of the vermouth, half of the thyme, and one of the chiles, shaking the pan to stir and coat them. Cover the pan with a lid, and allow the clams to cook for about 1–2 minutes, until they have opened. Over a large bowl, strain the clams, and set them aside, reserving the liquid. Cook the remaining clams in the same manner, using the remaining ingredients. Discard any unopened clams. As soon as they are cool enough to handle, remove the clams from their shells.

Return all of the clam liquid to the skillet and, over medium-high heat, reduce it for about 5 minutes, until it measures about 1 cup. Over medium-low heat, whisk in the garlic butter and cook until the liquid is bubbly and thickened.

Grill the bread according to the directions on page 8. Rub one side of each slice of bread with the garlic clove, and place on serving plates, garlic side up.

Add the clams to the sauce, and season with lemon juice, salt, and pepper, to taste. Cook for about 30 seconds, just long enough to rewarm the clams.

TO ASSEMBLE THE SANDWICHES: Arrange the clams over the bread. Pour about 3 tablespoons of the sauce over each sandwich, allowing it to run over the edges of the bread. Sprinkle the breadcrumbs over and top with the crisp garlic and the parsley leaves.

1 tablespoon extra-virgin olive oil
1 garlic clove, peeled
2 tablespoons finely grated
Parmigiano-Reggiano
1 tablespoon finely chopped
fresh Italian parsley leaves

4 slices white or whole-wheat sourdough bread (or see page 219)
1 garlic clove, peeled
20 fresh Italian parsley leaves

CHARRED RAPINI WITH WELSH RAREBIT AND BACON

Welsh rarebit, otherwise known as Welsh rabbit, is a sauce of melted cheese cooked with beer and mustard, traditionally poured over bread or crackers. As delicious as the first bite may be, an entire portion can be a little much. And so, to break up the monotony of this comforting cold-weather English dish, I add charred rapini with either some roasted tomatoes or applewood-smoked bacon. Rapini is a stalky green vegetable with small leaves and broccoli-like buds, also known as broccoli rabe or rape.

TO CHAR THE RAPINI: In a large bowl, toss together the rapini, olive oil, chile flakes, garlic, and salt. Allow to marinate about 5 minutes. Place the rapini on a hot grill, putting the stems over the hottest section of the grill. Grill for 3–5 minutes on each side, until it begins to blacken and char partially. Remove from the heat, discarding any of the pieces that are too blackened, and allow to cool.

Alternatively, to char on the stovetop: Heat a heavy-duty skillet over high heat. Add the rapini, and allow to char on one side for 7–10 minutes. Turn over, and char the other side. Remove from the skillet, discarding any of the pieces that are too blackened, and allow to cool.

Coarsely chop the rapini and set aside.

FOR THE BACON: In a small skillet, cook the bacon over medium heat until it's cooked all the way through but not crisp. Drain on a paper towel.

TO MAKE THE WELSH RAREBIT: Grill the bread according to the directions on page 8. Rub one side of each slice of bread with the garlic clove, and place on serving plates, garlic side up.

In a large bowl, combine the cheese with the starch. Rub the garlic clove over a medium-sized heavy-duty saucepan, and leave the clove in the pan. Pour the beer, chile flakes, and lemon juice into the saucepan and, over medium-low heat, bring to just below a simmer.

FOR THE RAPINI

1 bunch rapini, ¼ inch trimmed off ends of stalks

¼ cup extra-virgin olive oil

½ teaspoon dried chile flakes

1 garlic clove, peeled and finely chopped (about 1 teaspoon)

1 teaspoon kosher salt

2 slices thick-cut bacon, preferably applewood-smoked, cut diagonally into ¼-inch-wide pieces

or

1 recipe Roasted Tomatoes (see page 50), substituting 2 tablespoons extra-virgin olive oil for the chickpea oil

4 slices white or whole-wheat sourdough bread (or see page 219)

1 garlic clove, peeled

FOR THE WELSH RAREBIT

About 5 cups (1 pound) grated white Cheddar, preferably English, Keen's, or Montgomery

1 tablespoon potato starch or cornstarch

1 garlic clove, peeled and smashed

Add the cheese, one handful at a time, stirring in a figure-eight pattern, waiting for each handful to melt before adding the next. The mixture will thicken, but should still be thin enough to pour. Whisk in the pepper, mustard, and Worcestershire sauce, and add more lemon juice, to taste. Stir in the parsley, and remove the garlic clove and discard.

Immediately pour the Welsh rarebit sauce onto the bread, allowing it to run over the edges. Pile an uneven layer of rapini, leaving a 1-inch border of sauce. Scatter the bacon or tomatoes over the top. Eat right away so the texture of the sauce remains smooth.

1 cup beer, preferably pilsner or lager
Pinch of red chile flakes
2–3 teaspoons fresh lemon juice
Freshly cracked black pepper, to taste
2 tablespoons whole-grain mustard
8 drops Worcestershire sauce
2 tablespoons finely chopped
fresh Italian parsley leaves

GORGONZOLA, RADICCHIO, HONEY, AND WALNUTS

My affinity for this sandwich dates back to a hot and sticky afternoon in Florence. After hours of looking for an open restaurant during the desolate month of August, we finally stumbled upon a little wine bar that served salads and sandwiches all day long.

Though I had eaten the combination of ingredients in other forms, I had never thought to combine Gorgonzola, radicchio, and honey on a sandwich until I had it that day at Enoteca Baldovino. Choose a honey that isn't too floral, such as buckwheat or chestnut, and look for the slightly softer and milder Gorgonzola Dolce at an Italian deli or cheese shop. Though you won't need a full recipe of the Candied Spicy Walnuts, they're so good that I'm sure they won't go to waste. And if you're in a hurry, you can simply toast the nuts and skip the candying, although you'll be missing out on a real treat.

1 recipe Roasted Radicchio
(see page 40)
4 slices walnut, white, or whole-wheat sourdough bread
(or see page 219)
8 ounces Gorgonzola Dolce
Approximately 3 tablespoons honey, preferably buckwheat or chestnut
1 recipe Candied Spicy Walnuts
(see page 192), leaving 8 halves whole and coarsely chopping
the remainder
Approximately 1 bunch chives, minced

Coarsely chop the roasted radicchio.

TO ASSEMBLE THE SANDWICHES: Grill the bread according to the instructions on page 8. Place the slices on serving plates.

Spread an uneven layer of the Gorgonzola over each slice of bread, and spoon about 2 teaspoons of honey over the cheese. Scatter about a ¼ cup of chopped walnuts over each, and evenly distribute the radicchio, leaving a border of the Gorgonzola around the edge. Sprinkle the sandwiches with chives, and place 2 candied walnut halves overlapping in the center of each.

Olive-Oil-Poached Albacore Tuna, Rémoulade, and Cheddar Cheese

Between you and me, this is just a fancy name for a tuna melt. The only difference is that this one tastes good. It's not made with flavorless canned tuna packed in water and mixed with sweet mayonnaise-style salad dressing. Nor is the tuna warm and browned around the edges and hiding underneath an oozing slab of bright-orange processed cheese.

This sandwich is made with fresh albacore tuna poached in extra-virgin olive oil and then combined with homemade rémoulade. Crumble your favorite farmhouse Cheddar over the sandwich, and leave it under the broiler just long enough to melt the cheese. Feel free to call it a tuna melt, but I think you'll agree it doesn't taste like any other.

TO POACH THE ALBACORE: Place the rosemary, bay leaves, and lemon slices on the bottom of a medium saucepan. Arrange the albacore on top, and pour over the oil to cover completely. Sprinkle with salt and pepper. Cook over low heat for about 8–10 minutes, until the first bubble appears in the oil. (It should still be cool enough to be able to dip your finger in it.)

Immediately remove the pan from the heat, flip each piece of fish over, and cover the pan with a lid. Allow the tuna to sit in the warm oil for about 5–10 minutes, until it's cooked all the way through. Remove the tuna and refrigerate. Strain the oil and chill to room temperature to use in the rémoulade.

Prepare the Rémoulade with the cooled poaching oil according to the directions on page 207.

Place the tuna in a medium bowl and, using your fingers, flake it into large chunks. Add ¾ cup of the rémoulade, and mix to combine. Season

FOR THE ALBACORE TUNA

1 3-inch branch fresh rosemary

2 bay leaves

½ lemon, cut into 4 ½-inch-thick slices, plus extra lemon for squeezing over tuna

12 ounces fresh albacore tuna, sliced into ¾-inch-thick fillets

2 cups extra-virgin olive oil

2 teaspoons kosher salt

½ teaspoon freshly cracked black pepper

1 recipe Rémoulade (see page 207) made with the olive oil from the poached tuna instead of vegetable oil

4 slices white or whole-wheat sourdough bread (or see page 219)

1 garlic clove, peeled

4 ounces white Cheddar, such as Grafton, Strauss Family, Bravo, or Montgomery

Approximately 1 bunch fresh chives, minced

with salt, pepper, and lemon juice to taste. If you like, add the remaining rémoulade.

Adjust the oven rack to the upper position, and preheat the broiler.

Grill the bread according to the directions on page 8. Rub one side of each slice of bread with the garlic clove, and place on a baking sheet, garlic side up.

TO ASSEMBLE THE SANDWICHES: Pile the tuna unevenly over the bread. Crumble the cheese and scatter unevenly over the center, leaving a 1-inch border of tuna around the edge. Heat under the broiler for about 30 seconds, until the cheese is melted. Squeeze a few drops of lemon juice over and sprinkle them with chives.

BAKED RICOTTA, SLOW-ROASTED ROMA TOMATOES, PESTO, AND GLAZED ONIONS

With the help of a little flour and eggs, fresh ricotta is transformed when baked. From its soft, creamy origins, it solidifies into a firm and dense cheese. If possible, buy your ricotta fresh from a local cheesemaker, cheese store, or Italian deli. Don't worry if tomatoes aren't at their late-summer peak; this is a sandwich you can make most of the year. Though most varieties aren't worth buying after summer, you can find decent Romas year-round. And when roasted for several hours, they become concentrated and sweeten up tenfold.

Drizzle the baked ricotta with a spoonful of pesto, nestle the glazed red onions alongside the slow-roasted tomatoes, and even your meat-loving friends will devour this satisfying sandwich.

TO ROAST THE TOMATOES: Adjust the oven racks to the lower and middle positions, and preheat the oven to 200 degrees.

Oil a baking sheet with the olive oil, and sprinkle it with salt. Place the tomatoes, cut side down, on the baking sheet, and slide a small sprig of rosemary under each half. Roast on the middle rack of the oven about $4\frac{1}{2}$ hours, until the tomatoes are no longer watery and have a glazed sheen. Turn them over, and roast for another 45 minutes to an hour, until the skin is caramelized.

(The tomatoes can be roasted 2–3 days in advance, stored in the refrigerator, and rewarmed.)

TO GLAZE THE ONIONS: Turn the oven up to 400 degrees.

Scatter half of the thyme sprigs over the bottom of a 10–12-inch oven-proof skillet. Drizzle the pan with 2 teaspoons of the balsamic vinegar and 2 tablespoons of the olive oil. Cut the onions in half through the root, and

FOR THE TOMATOES
1 tablespoon extra-virgin olive oil
$\frac{1}{2}$ teaspoon kosher salt
8 small to medium or 4 extra-large (about 1 pound total) Roma tomatoes, cut in half lengthwise
4–8 sprigs fresh rosemary

FOR THE ONIONS
20 3-inch sprigs fresh thyme
1 tablespoon balsamic vinegar
3 tablespoons extra-virgin olive oil
2 medium yellow or red onions
6 fresh sage or bay leaves
$\frac{1}{2}$ teaspoon kosher salt

FOR THE RICOTTA
$\frac{1}{2}$ cup unbleached all-purpose flour
2 cups (1 pound) fresh ricotta cheese
2 extra-large eggs
$\frac{3}{4}$ teaspoon kosher salt
Freshly cracked black pepper, to taste
$\frac{1}{4}$ cup (1 ounce) finely grated Parmigiano-Reggiano
2 tablespoons unsalted butter, melted and cooled
8 gratings fresh whole nutmeg

remove the skin. Trim the hairs of the root and, keeping the root intact, cut each onion into eighths. Arrange the onion pieces next to one another, flat side down, in a concentric circle. Place a whole sage or bay leaf in between every other onion wedge, sprinkle with salt, and scatter the remaining thyme sprigs over the onions. Drizzle them with the remaining oil and vinegar.

Roast the onions on the lower rack for about 35 minutes, until tender and caramelized. Flip over one of the onions to make sure they're well browned. If necessary, place the skillet over a high flame on the stovetop and cook the onions for about 2–3 more minutes, until they're well browned. Allow to cool.

TO MAKE THE RICOTTA: Sift the flour into a small bowl.

Over a large bowl, strain the ricotta through a ricer, food mill, or fine-mesh sieve. In another small bowl, beat the 2 eggs together lightly, then measure out ¼ cup plus 2 tablespoons of them and set aside. Discard the remaining beaten egg.

Make a well in the center of the ricotta, and pour in the egg. Add the salt, pepper, and Parmesan, and whisk together in the well. Slowly draw the ricotta into the egg mixture, stirring to incorporate. Whisk in the butter, and stir in the flour and nutmeg.

Transfer the mixture to a 9-inch glass pie pan or tart pan, spreading it out evenly. Bake on the middle rack for about 45 minutes to an hour, until nicely browned on top. Allow to cool, and cut the ricotta into 16 wedges.

Remove the onions from the skillet, and discard the herbs.

Grill the bread according to the directions on page 8. Rub one side of each slice of bread with the garlic clove, and cut each slice in half on the diagonal. Place the slices on serving plates, garlic side up.

TO ASSEMBLE THE SANDWICHES: Arrange 2 wedges of ricotta facing in opposite directions over each half-slice of bread with one slice on its side and the other slice bottom down. Spoon a tablespoon or so of pesto over the cheese. Place 2 wedges of onions, fanned out slightly, on top of the cheese, and nestle 2 tomatoes in between the onions. Shave 3 to 4 slices of Parmesan on each half.

1 recipe Parsley Basil Pesto
(see page 212)

4 slices white or whole-wheat sour-dough bread (or see page 219)
1 garlic clove, peeled
Approximately ¼-pound wedge
Parmigiano-Reggiano, for shaving
over the tops of the sandwiches

SPANISH FRIED EGGS, SALSA ROMESCO, AND SHEEP'S MILK CHEESE

It was in a Spanish hotel, in the middle of my complimentary buffet breakfast, that I realized my own grandmother knew how to fry the perfect egg. Unlike the French, who fry their eggs more slowly in warm butter, my grandmother cooked hers fast in hot oil. Crispy around the edges, with a soft and runny yolk, those Spanish fried eggs looked just like hers. Once you've tasted them fried in olive oil, it's hard to make them any other way.

4 slices white or whole-wheat sourdough bread (or see page 219)

1 garlic clove, peeled

1 Recipe Salsa Romesco
(see page 210)

½ cup extra-virgin olive oil

4 extra-large eggs

Fleur de sel or kosher salt, to taste

Freshly cracked black pepper, to taste

Approximately ¼-pound wedge
Spanish sheep's-milk cheese, such
as Manchego or Queso Roncal,
for shaving over the top of
the sandwiches

Grill the bread according to the directions on page 8. Rub one side of each slice of bread with the garlic clove, and place the slices on serving plates, garlic side up. Spread each slice of bread unevenly with about 3 tablespoons of the salsa romesco.

In a 4-inch cast-iron or heavy-duty skillet, heat the oil over high heat until very hot but not smoking. To test if the oil is hot enough, place a drop of water in the oil. If it spatters instantly, the oil is ready.

Crack an egg into a bowl to check that the yolk isn't broken. Pour the egg into the hot oil, sprinkle with fleur de sel, and allow to cook for about 1–2 minutes, until the whites are bubbly and the outer edge becomes brown and crisp. Just before it's done, spoon a little of the oil onto the yolk to create an opaque film over it. Remove the egg, and place it on the center of a slice of bread. Heat the oil, and continue frying the eggs in the same manner, adding more oil if necessary. Sprinkle with fleur de sel and pepper, and top with 6–8 shavings of cheese.

CLOSED-FACED SANDWICHES

If you find the open-faced sandwich too complex, the tea sandwich too fussy, the sort-of sandwich too abstract, and the dessert sandwich too sweet, then the closed-faced sandwich is the one for you. Sandwiched between buttery grilled bread, these traditional combinations will transport you to another time, another place. Whether it's a fried-oyster sandwich in New Orleans, a pan bagna on the French Riviera, or a Monte Cristo in a fancy hotel coffee shop, I'm sure you'll have memories to go along with each bite.

Simple and straightforward, these closed-faced ensembles require no complicated techniques. Some, such as the Classic Grilled Cheese or the Reuben, are assembled first and then grilled to warm the ingredients and melt the cheese inside. Others, such as the Fried Egg Sandwich and the PLT, call for their bread to be pre-toasted or pre-grilled so as not to disturb or heat up the fillings inside.

No matter where the craving strikes, these two-handed combos promise to satisfy and comfort you like nothing else.

GRILLED CHEESE SANDWICHES

Cheese is a magical food. Rich, salty, and fortifying, it satisfies a craving as nothing else can. When melted, its magic is magnified ten times; heat transforms the cheese's solid, dense texture into a pliable, smooth consistency and causes the sharp, rich flavors to become even more pronounced and delicious.

A grilled-cheese sandwich is the ultimate foray into the world of hot cheese. My addiction to this American classic began in my junior-high-school cafeteria, where I would patiently await the hot square package: a grease-stained paper envelope concealing a freshly made combo of white bread, margarine, and processed American cheese melted to perfection. Though my tastes have become more sophisticated, the simplest and what I call "classic" version of a grilled cheese is still my favorite.

For the Classic Grilled Cheese, you'll need just three ingredients: butter, bread, and cheese. Choose your cheese carefully, since not all varieties are suitable for this simple sandwich. Many grilled-cheese aficiona-dos swear by the sharp twang of an aged Cheddar, but I stand by the deep, strong flavors of Gruyère or Swiss Emmenthaler. An aged Cheddar's dry and dense texture just can't compete when it comes to that stretchy meltability of Gruyère.

Cheeses that are creamy and soft, such as a triple-crème Brie, Roquefort, or Reblochon, won't hold up to the cooking heat and will make an unwanted cheesy mess that oozes out of the bread and onto your grill. These types are best when spread directly on top of a slice of grilled bread (see the simplest open-faced sandwiches). Avoid fresh-style cheeses, like feta and queso fresco, which are better used when cold and crumbled over something as a topping. Hard-style cheeses, such as Parmigiano-Reggiano, Pecorino, and Manchego, are tasty, but I prefer them shaved over an open-faced sandwich. Whichever cheese you choose, remember that, when it comes to cheeses, too much of a good thing can be too much. A few thin slices of a robust, tangy cheese are enough to add flavor to your buttery toasted bread, without turning it into a sickeningly rich experience.

Though I'm still a purist at heart, every now and then I want a more substantial grilled-cheese sandwich. The smallest additions can bring something to a grilled cheese without taking away from its simple purity. A dollop of whole-grain mustard and a smattering of marinated onions will turn the Classic Grilled Cheese into a completely new sandwich experience. Add a few slices of ham and a fried egg, and—*voilà*—you've made that Parisian favorite, a Croque Madame. Leave off the egg and pour some cheesy Mornay sauce over it and you've made a Croque Monsieur.

Though I'm much older now and have grown up in my taste for cheese, I still love sinking my teeth into the buttery, crisp bread and watching the hot cheese interior stretch away, revealing the wonderfully strange and stringy afterlife of melted cheese.

CLASSIC GRILLED CHEESE

TO ASSEMBLE THE SANDWICHES: Set half of the bread slices buttered side down, and cover them with the cheese slices, folding them over if they extend past the edges of the bread. Place the top slice of bread over the cheese, buttered side up.

Grill the sandwiches according to the directions on page 8 and cut each in half on the diagonal.

8 slices white or whole-wheat sour-dough bread (or see page 219)
8 ounces Gruyère cheese, sliced into 24–32 ⅟₁₆-inch-thick slices

SUMMERTIME GRILLED CHEESE VARIATION

When tomatoes are in season, my friend Jason Asch insists that I make his grilled-cheese sandwich with the tomato slices layered inside before it's grilled. Though I make this exception for him and for him only, I prefer the firm texture of the tomato when it's slipped in after the sandwich is already grilled.

2–4 tomatoes, sliced ¼ inch thick, core end discarded
1–2 tablespoons extra-virgin olive oil
Kosher salt, to taste

Drizzle olive oil over the tomato slices and sprinkle with salt. Allow to sit for about five minutes.

Assemble and grill the sandwiches according to the directions above. Cut each sandwich in half on the diagonal and slide in the tomatoes.

CLASSIC GRILLED CHEESE WITH MARINATED ONIONS AND WHOLE-GRAIN MUSTARD

Though this variation on the Classic Grilled Cheese calls for only a few extra ingredients, it's a completely different sandwich. The onions and mustard salute the sensibilities of Alsace, in the northern region of France, imparting a tangy zeal to this basic cheese sandwich.

TO PREPARE THE MARINATED ONIONS: In a medium bowl, combine the oil, vinegar, salt, and pepper. Add the onions, toss to coat them, and allow to marinate for 15–20 minutes at room temperature. Season them with more vinegar, salt, and pepper, to taste.

TO ASSEMBLE THE SANDWICHES: Set half of the slices of bread buttered side down. Spread an even layer of mustard over the bread and cover with half the cheese slices, folding them back in toward the middle if they extend past the edges of the bread. Scatter the marinated onions on top and place the remaining cheese slices over the onions. Put the top slices of bread over the cheese, buttered side up.

Grill the sandwiches according to the directions on page 8.

Cut each sandwich in half on the diagonal.

FOR THE ONIONS

⅓ cup extra-virgin olive oil

2–3 tablespoons champagne vinegar or white-wine vinegar

2 tablespoons kosher salt

1 tablespoon freshly cracked black pepper

2 medium yellow onions, sliced into ⅛-inch-thick slices

8 slices white or whole-wheat sourdough bread (or see page 219)

¼ cup whole-grain mustard

8 ounces Gruyère cheese, sliced into 24–32 ¹⁄₁₆-inch-thick slices

CROQUE MADAME

Why Madame? Because it has an egg, of course.

TO ASSEMBLE THE SANDWICHES: Set half of the slices of bread buttered side down, and cover them with the cheese slices, folding them back in toward the middle if they extend past the edges of the bread. Place 3 or 4 slices of the ham in an even layer over the cheese, and place the top slice of bread over the ham, buttered side up.

Grill the sandwiches according to the directions on page 8 and place on serving plates.

TO FRY THE EGGS: Crack two eggs into two separate bowls to check that the yolks aren't broken. In 2 6-inch non-stick skillets, melt half of the butter over medium-high heat, until it starts to bubble. Pour 1 egg into each pan, being careful not to break the yolks. Add a teaspoon of water to each pan, sprinkle the eggs with fleur de sel, and cover the pans with lids. Cook the eggs for about 3 minutes for a soft-cooked egg and 5–6 minutes if you like your eggs firm. Wipe out the skillets, and fry the other 2 eggs in the remaining butter in the same manner. Center a fried egg over each of the grilled sandwiches and sprinkle with pepper.

8 slices white or whole-wheat sourdough bread (or see page 219)

8 ounces Gruyère cheese, sliced into 24–32 $\frac{1}{16}$-inch-thick slices

12 ounces smoked ham, such as Black Forest, sliced into 12–16 $\frac{1}{16}$-inch-thick slices

4 extra-large eggs

3 tablespoons unsalted butter

Fleur de sel or kosher salt, to taste

Freshly cracked black pepper, to taste

CROQUE MONSIEUR

The male counterpart to the Croque Madame is made in the same manner, but instead of a fried egg on top, it gets a warm and creamy Mornay sauce.

TO MAKE THE MORNAY SAUCE: In a medium saucepan, over medium heat, melt the butter. Add the onion, salt, and cracked peppercorns, and cook about 10 minutes, until the onion is soft but has not begun to color.

Remove from the heat, and add the flour in 2 batches, whisking to combine it with the onion and butter. Return the pan to the stove, and over low heat, cook a few minutes, until the flour is absorbed, stirring constantly so that it doesn't brown. Remove from the heat, and slowly whisk in the milk and add the bay leaf. Return the pan to the stove, and bring the mixture to a boil. Reduce the heat to low and simmer, stirring occasionally to prevent the sauce from burning on the bottom of the pan. Cook for 20–30 minutes, until the taste of raw flour is gone and the mixture is thick, smooth, and silky. If it's too thick and becoming difficult to stir, you'll need to whisk in a little more milk.

Using a fine-mesh sieve, strain the sauce. Wash and dry the pan, and pour the sauce back into it. Over low heat, add the 2 cheeses, a little at a time, stirring until they're completely melted.

Adjust the oven rack to the upper position, and preheat the broiler.

TO ASSEMBLE THE SANDWICHES: Set half of the slices of bread buttered side down, and cover them with the Gruyère cheese slices, folding them back in toward the middle if they extend past the edges of the bread. Place 3 to 4 slices of ham in an even layer over the cheese, and put the top slice of bread over the ham, buttered side up.

Grill the sandwiches according to the directions on page 8.

Place the sandwiches on a baking sheet and spoon the Mornay sauce over them, leaving a 1-inch border of bread. Heat under the broiler for a minute or two, until the sauce is bubbling. Sprinkle the chives over the sandwiches.

FOR THE MORNAY SAUCE

2 tablespoons unsalted butter

4 tablespoons finely chopped yellow onion

Pinch of kosher salt

4 black peppercorns, cracked

2 tablespoons unbleached all-purpose flour

2 cups whole milk

1 bay leaf

½ cup (approximately 2 ounces) finely grated Gruyère cheese

¼ cup (1 ounce) finely grated Parmigiano-Reggiano

8 slices white or whole-wheat sourdough bread (or see page 219)

8 ounces Gruyère cheese, sliced into 24–32 $\frac{1}{16}$-inch-thick slices

12 ounces smoked ham, such as Black Forest, sliced into 12–16 $\frac{1}{16}$-inch-thick slices

1 bunch fresh chives, minced

Ham, Creamed Spinach, and Stewed Leeks

Creaming and stewing can make just about anything taste more delicious, especially the leeks and spinach on this version of a Croque Monsieur.

FOR THE LEEKS: Slice the leeks on the bias into ¼-inch-thick pieces. Rinse the pieces under cold water, and pat them dry.

In a medium skillet, over medium-low heat, melt the butter until it begins to bubble. Add the leeks, and cook about 5 minutes, stirring occasionally, until they're wilted. Add the shallots, parsley, and wine, and bring to a boil. Turn the heat down, cover the skillet, and reduce the mixture by half. Add the water and salt, and reduce the mixture by half again.

TO MAKE THE CREAMED SPINACH: In a medium saucepan, over medium heat, cook the spinach in a few tablespoons of water until it's completely wilted. Drain and allow it to cool, then squeeze out the excess water with your hands or in a dish towel. Finely chop the spinach, and set it aside.

In a medium saucepan, melt the butter over medium heat. Add the onion, salt, and pepper, and cook about 10 minutes, until the onion is soft but has not begun to color.

Remove the pan from the heat, and add the flour in 2 batches, whisking to combine it with the onion and butter. Return the pan to the stove, and cook over low heat for a few minutes, until the flour is absorbed, stirring constantly so that it doesn't brown. Remove from the heat, and slowly whisk in the milk and add the bay leaf. Return the pan to the stove and bring the mixture to a boil. Reduce the heat to low and simmer, stirring occasionally to prevent the sauce from burning on the bottom of the pan. Cook for 20–30 minutes, until the taste of raw flour is gone and the mixture is thick, smooth, and silky. If it's too thick and becoming difficult to stir, you'll need to whisk in a little more milk.

Using a fine-mesh sieve, strain the sauce. Measure out ½ cup of the

FOR THE LEEKS

4 leeks, root ends trimmed, dark-green tops cut off and discarded

1 stick (4 ounces) unsalted butter

2 shallots, peeled and finely chopped (about ½ cup)

1 tablespoon finely chopped fresh Italian parsley leaves

¼ cup dry white wine

¼ cup water

1 tablespoon kosher salt

FOR THE CREAMED SPINACH

¾ pound fresh spinach (3–4 bunches), washed, dried, and stems removed

2 tablespoons unsalted butter

4 tablespoons finely chopped yellow onion

Kosher salt, to taste

4 black peppercorns, cracked

2 tablespoons all-purpose flour

1½ cups whole milk

1 bay leaf

¾ cup heavy cream

8 slices white or whole-wheat sourdough bread (or see page 219)

sauce and set it aside. Wash and dry the pan, and pour the remaining sauce back into it. Add the spinach and cream, and bring to a low boil over medium heat. Turn the heat down to low, and simmer for about 15 minutes to thicken slightly, stirring occasionally.

Adjust the oven rack to the upper position, and preheat the broiler.

TO ASSEMBLE THE SANDWICHES: Set half of the slices buttered side down, and cover with the cheese slices, folding them back over if they extend past the edges of the bread. Place an even layer of ham slices over the cheese, spoon 3–4 tablespoons of the creamed spinach over, and place a layer of leeks over. Put the top slice of bread on the sandwich, buttered side up.

Grill the sandwiches according to the directions on page 8.

Place the sandwiches on a baking sheet, and spoon the reserved sauce over the top of each, leaving a 1-inch border of bread. Sprinkle them with the grated Gruyère, and heat under the broiler for a minute or two, until the sauce is bubbling and browned.

4 ounces Gruyère cheese, sliced
into 12–16 $\frac{1}{16}$-inch-thick slices
12 ounces smoked ham, such
as Black Forest, sliced into
12–16 $\frac{1}{16}$-inch-thick slices
About $\frac{1}{2}$ cup (2 ounces) finely grated
Gruyère cheese, for sprinkling
over the sandwiches

AUTOSTRADA SANDWICH

The Italians know how to eat. They even take their road food seriously. When driving around Italy, I often need a break from those high-speed Italian roads, so I always stop at the convenient auto-grille, the Italian equivalent of our truck stop, for a quick grilled sandwich and a cheap glass of red wine.

Salty and rich, this classic Autostrada Sandwich is grilled with four kinds of cured meats, provolone cheese, and chopped cherry pepper for a spicy zing. It is the perfect mid-day snack.

TO ASSEMBLE THE SANDWICHES: Set half of the slices of bread buttered side down, and cover them with half of the cheese slices, folding them back in toward the middle if they extend past the edges of the bread. Scatter the peppers evenly over the cheese. Place a single layer of mortadella over the peppers, followed by a layer of coppa, a layer of salami, and a layer of prosciutto. Place one more slice of cheese over the meats. (As you layer the cheese and meats, be sure to cover the bread and allow some of the meat to extend just beyond the edge of the bread so it gets crisp while grilling.) Put the top slice of bread over, buttered side up.

Grill the sandwiches according to the directions on page 8.

Cut each sandwich in half on the diagonal.

8 slices white or whole-wheat sour-dough bread (or see page 219)

4 ounces aged provolone, preferably imported, sliced into 6–10 $\frac{1}{16}$-inch-thick slices

4 ounces mortadella, preferably imported, sliced into 6–8 $\frac{1}{16}$-inch-thick slices and cut in half

4 ounces coppa, sliced into 16–20 $\frac{1}{16}$-inch-thick slices

4 ounces dry salami, such as soprossata, sliced into 16–20 $\frac{1}{16}$-inch-thick slices

2 ounces prosciutto, thinly sliced into about 8 slices

4 jarred marinated cherry peppers, seeded and finely chopped

FRIED OYSTER SANDWICH

Every once in a while, I eat something that I really love, something that I can't stop thinking about until I finally make it myself. The last time this happened was at Pearl Oyster Bar in New York City, where I had the perfect fried-oyster sandwich. When I got back to Campanile, I described the sandwich to our sous-chef, Dan Trudeau, who helped me come up with this perfect West Coast version.

For the freshest oysters, go to a reliable fishmonger who sells them already shucked. Choose medium-sized oysters from cold Northern water, and avoid Gulf oysters. Slathered with tangy mayonnaise, every bite of this sandwich should leave the corners of your mouth dripping with rémoulade. Serve it with a side of Creamy Coleslaw (see page 104) and you won't be able to stop thinking about this sandwich either.

20 oysters, such as Malpeque or
Hama Hama, shucked
¾ cup buttermilk
2 cups unbleached all-purpose flour
2 cups fine cornmeal
or semolina flour
¼ teaspoon cayenne pepper
1 teaspoon kosher salt, to taste
½ teaspoon freshly cracked
black pepper
4 store-bought hot-dog buns,
or homemade (see page 224)
1 recipe Clarified Butter
(see page 201)
1 recipe Rémoulade (see page 207)

In a small bowl, combine the oysters and buttermilk, and set aside to soak for 5 minutes.

In another small bowl, combine the flour, cornmeal, cayenne, salt, and pepper.

Over medium-high heat, heat a large cast-iron or heavy-duty skillet. If the hot-dog buns aren't sliced, slice them horizontally through the center, not cutting all the way through. Open the buns and brush a thin layer of the clarified butter on the inside. Toast them in the skillet, buttered sides down, for a few minutes, until they're golden brown.

Place the buns right side up on the serving plates. Spread a heaping tablespoon of rémoulade over each half of each bun.

Wipe out the skillet. Add ½ cup of the clarified butter to the skillet, and heat it over medium-high heat. Dredge the oysters in the flour mixture, thoroughly coating them. When the butter is very hot and almost smoking, fry the oysters about 3–4 minutes on each side, until they're crisp and golden brown. (Depending on the size of your pan, you may have to fry the oysters in 2 or 3 batches.) Place the oysters on a paper towel to drain.

TO ASSEMBLE THE SANDWICHES: Place 5 oysters in each bun.

MONTE CRISTO

I wrote this recipe for the generation that didn't grow up eating this fifties classic. Believe it or not, turkey, ham, cheese, and strawberry jam is not as awful as it sounds. Once you try it, you'll choose this deep-fried retro combo as your special-occasion sandwich too. Pile the crispy wedges onto a platter, dust with powdered sugar, and watch to see who fights over the last piece.

TO MAKE THE BATTER: In a medium bowl, combine the flour, corn-starch, baking powder, baking soda, cayenne, and salt. Whisk in the club soda and beer. The mixture should be the consistency of pancake batter. Refriger-ate until you're ready to use it.

TO ASSEMBLE THE SANDWICHES: Set half of the slices buttered side down, and cover with the cheese slices, folding them over if they extend past the edges. Layer the ham and turkey over the cheese, and spread the jam over the turkey. Place the top slice of bread on, buttered side up.

Grill the sandwiches according to the directions on page 8.

Pour the oil into a deep heavy-duty saucepan to fill it halfway. Heat the oil to 350 degrees, measuring the temperature on a deep-fat thermometer.

Cut the sandwiches on a diagonal into thirds, to make 9 triangular pieces.

Stir the batter. Dip each sandwich piece into the batter, thoroughly coat-ing it. Fry the pieces 2 or 3 at a time, being careful not to overcrowd them in the pan. Cook them for about 3 minutes on each side, until they're nicely browned, and transfer to a paper towel to drain. Allow the oil to come back up to temperature before you fry the next batch of sandwiches.

Place the sandwiches on a platter. Sift a very heavy layer of powdered sugar over them, and serve with a side of jam.

YIELD: 9 pieces

FOR THE BATTER

2 cups unbleached all-purpose flour

1 cup cornstarch

1 tablespoon baking powder

1 tablespoon baking soda

¼ teaspoon cayenne pepper

1 teaspoon kosher salt

½ cup club soda

1½ cups dark beer

6 slices white or whole-wheat sour-dough bread (or see page 219)

6 ounces Gruyère cheese, sliced into 18 ⅟₁₆-inch-thick slices

8 ounces smoked ham, such as Black Forest, sliced into 9 ⅟₁₆-inch-thick slices

8 ounces roast turkey, sliced into 9 ⅟₁₆-inch-thick slices

3 tablespoons strawberry jam, plus extra to serve on the side

Vegetable oil, for deep-frying

½ cup powdered sugar

'ino's Pancetta, Lettuce, and Tomato

My favorite American sandwich is a BLT, yet it almost didn't make it into this book; the world doesn't need another recipe for it. But after eating at 'ino, a tiny sandwich shop in Greenwich Village in New York, I decided their version—a PLT—was a different story.

P is for pancetta, sold at Italian delis and upscale markets. Cut from a large salami-like roll, it is the Italian version of bacon, unsmoked and cured with salt and spices.

This is strictly a seasonal sandwich; I forbid you to make it at any time except when tomatoes are at their prime—ripe, juicy, and sweet.

1 recipe Lemon Aïoli (see page 204)

8 ounces pancetta, sliced into 16 ¼-inch-thick slices

1 tablespoon extra-virgin olive oil, for drizzling over the tomatoes

2 or 3 ripe tomatoes, core end discarded, sliced into ¼-inch-thick slices

½ teaspoon kosher salt

8 slices white or whole-wheat sourdough bread (or see page 219)

1 garlic clove, peeled

Approximately 2 cups arugula leaves, loosely packed (about 1 to 1½ ounces)

Adjust the oven rack to the middle position, and preheat the oven to 350 degrees.

Place the slices of pancetta about ½ inch apart from each other on a baking sheet. Cook them for about 20 minutes, until they're cooked through, but not crisp.

Drizzle the olive oil over the tomato slices, and sprinkle them with salt. Allow them to sit for 5–10 minutes.

Grill the bread according to the directions on page 8.

TO ASSEMBLE THE SANDWICHES: Spoon about 1 tablespoon of the lemon aïoli on one side of each slice of bread. Arrange the slices of pancetta on the bottom slices of bread, and place the tomato slices over it. Arrange the arugula on top and cover with the top slice of bread. Cut each sandwich in half on the diagonal.

PAN BAGNA

Inspired by the salty sea and heat of the summer sun, this classic tuna sandwich marries all the flavors of the Mediterranean. Tomatoes, tuna, hard-cooked eggs, cucumbers, anchovies, and olives are nestled together and generously bathed in a fresh herb vinaigrette.

For my Pan Bagna, I poach fillets of albacore tuna in olive oil, but if you don't have time, there are plenty of good imported olive-oil-packed tunas on the market. Try to find salt-packed anchovies, usually sold by the piece at Italian delis and specialty stores. If you're an anchovy lover like me, add some extra pieces inside of the sandwich.

If you don't want to bathe yourself in olive oil while eating this sandwich, you'll need to learn my pan-bagna stance: hold the sandwich with two hands, stick out your rear end as far as you can, lean forward, and dig in, letting all the juices drip in front of you, directly onto the floor.

If you're going to make your own buns, you may as well make a whole batch and freeze the extra baked buns for another time. Or buy round Italian-style rolls at your local bakery or market.

1 recipe Crusty White Loaf dough (see page 219), shaped into pan-bagna rolls (see page 221) or 4 store-bought soft rolls

2 extra-large eggs

1 recipe poached albacore tuna (see page 76), or 12 ounces imported tuna packed in olive oil

24–32 olives (approximately 4 ounces), preferably Nyons or Niçoise, with the pits removed, or ½ cup Tapenade (see page 211)

1 recipe Salsa Verde (see page 213)

4 3-inch-long salt-packed anchovies, rinsed well, backbone removed

1 teaspoon finely chopped lemon zest

2 tablespoons extra-virgin olive oil (optional)

1 tablespoon finely chopped fresh Italian parsley leaves

2 medium ripe tomatoes, core end discarded, sliced into ¼-inch-thick slices

1 teaspoon kosher salt

1 medium Japanese or Persian cucumber, sliced on the extreme diagonal into ¼-inch-thick slices

Freshly cracked black pepper, to taste

TO HARD-COOK THE EGGS: Place the eggs in a small saucepan with water to cover. Bring them to a boil over high heat, and turn the heat down to a low simmer. Simmer 7 minutes, and immediately plunge the eggs into a large bowl of ice water to chill.

Flake the tuna into large chunks, and place in a bowl. If you're using olives, add them to the tuna and pour 3 tablespoons of the salsa verde over it, tossing to coat. Allow the tuna to marinate for about 20 minutes.

Place the anchovies on a plate and sprinkle them with the lemon zest, a tablespoon of the tuna-poaching oil, or extra-virgin olive oil, and the parsley. Allow them to marinate for about 20 minutes.

Drizzle a tablespoon of the tuna-poaching oil or extra-virgin olive oil over the tomato slices, and sprinkle them with salt. Allow them to sit for 5–10 minutes.

TO ASSEMBLE THE SANDWICHES: Slice the rolls in half horizontally. Generously brush both halves of each roll with salsa verde. Spoon the tuna over one half of the roll, being sure to include a few olives (or some tape-nade). Peel the eggs and, using an egg slicer, cut them into ¼-inch-thick slices. Or just cut the eggs into quarters. Arrange the egg slices on top of the tuna, and place a layer of anchovies over. Put the tomato slices on the anchovies, and spoon a tablespoon of the salsa verde over them. Layer the cucumber slices on top, and sprinkle some freshly cracked black pepper over them. Place the top half of the roll on, and allow the sandwiches to sit for 5–10 minutes so the flavors have a chance to meld.

Try to resist cutting the sandwiches in half.

Dan's Sicilian Waldorf Sandwich

Dan Trudeau, our sous-chef at Campanile, prefers his Sicilian rendition of Waldorf salad to the overly sweet American version. Dan replaced the grapes with dried currants, and the walnuts with toasted pine nuts. And as for the marshmallows, forget about them. For the most succulent and tender chicken ever, marinate it first in our spiced brine for at least 24 hours and up to 2 days.

TO MAKE THE BRINE: In a small non-reactive pot, combine 2 cups of the water, the kosher salt, sugar, bay leaves, thyme, allspice, juniper berries, and cloves. Bring the mixture to a boil over high heat, and remove it from the heat. Add 4 more cups of water, and allow it to cool to room temperature. Refrigerate the brine until it's well chilled, at least 2 hours.

Place the chicken in the brine. It should be completely immersed in liq-uid; if not, add a little more water. Cover and refrigerate, allowing the chicken to marinate in the brine for at least 24 hours and up to 2 days.

TO ROAST THE CHICKEN: Adjust the oven rack to the middle position, and preheat the oven to 400 degrees.

FOR THE BRINE
Approximately 6–8 cups water
½ cup plus 2 tablespoons kosher salt
⅓ cup sugar
2 bay leaves
1 tablespoon dried thyme
1 teaspoon cracked whole allspice
½ teaspoon crushed juniper berries
3 whole cloves

1 3-pound whole fryer or small roasting chicken, rinsed well
2 tablespoons vegetable oil, for rubbing on the skin

FOR THE MAYONNAISE
1 extra-large egg yolk
1 teaspoon kosher salt, or to taste

Pat the chicken dry, and rub the skin with vegetable oil. Roast it in a baking dish for about 1 hour, until the juices run clear when the thigh joint is pierced with a knife. Allow the chicken to cool completely.

Remove the skin and discard (or eat). Pull the meat off the bones, shredding it into medium-sized pieces. You should have about 3 cups of chicken meat to use.

TO MAKE THE MAYONNAISE: In the bowl of an electric mixer or in a medium-sized stainless-steel bowl, whisk the egg yolk, salt, and mustard by hand. Slowly drizzle in the oil, drop by drop, whisking constantly. As the mixture begins to thicken, add a teaspoon of the lemon juice and a teaspoon of water.

Once you've added almost half of the oil, place the bowl in the mixer fitted with a whisk attachment and mix on medium speed, or continue to whisk in the oil by hand. Pour the oil in a slow, steady trickle, scraping down the sides of the bowl as necessary. As the mixture thickens, add a little more of the lemon juice, vinegar, and water, and continue whisking until the remaining oil is completely incorporated and the sauce is thickened. Season with lemon juice and salt, to taste.

TO TOAST THE PINE NUTS: Adjust the oven rack to the middle position, and preheat the oven to 325 degrees. Spread the pine nuts on a baking sheet, and toast them in the oven for about 8 minutes, until they're lightly browned. Allow them to cool.

In a large bowl, combine the chicken and $1/2$–1 cup of the mayonnaise, to taste. Add the pine nuts, celery, currants, parsley, and lemon juice, and toss with your hands to combine the ingredients. Season the salad with salt, pepper, and lemon juice to taste.

Grill the bread according to the directions on page 8.

TO ASSEMBLE THE SANDWICHES: Spoon about 1–2 tablespoons of the mayonnaise over half of the bread slices. Arrange the chicken salad on top and cover with the top slice of bread. Cut each sandwich in half on the diagonal.

$1/2$ teaspoon Dijon mustard

1 cup vegetable oil

1 tablespoon lemon juice

1–2 teaspoons water

$1/2$ cup pine nuts

1 celery stalk, cut into $1/4$-inch dice

$1/2$ cup dried currants

$1/4$ cup finely chopped fresh Italian parsley leaves

2–3 tablespoons fresh lemon juice

Kosher salt, to taste

Freshly cracked black pepper, to taste

8 slices white or whole-wheat sourdough bread (or see page 219)

FRENCH BAGUETTE WITH BUTTER AND PROSCIUTTO

If I'm ever stranded on a desert island with only three ingredients, I pray that they are prosciutto, butter, and baguette. Minimalist in appearance, yet concentrated in flavor, this sleek sandwich is surprisingly satisfying.

Think of it as a ham-and-sort-of-cheese sandwich. Since butter takes the place of cheese, choose your butter with discretion. Imported butters or domestic farmhouse-style butters are richer and sweeter and balance the saltiness of the ham. For the ham, I prefer either an imported prosciutto di Parma, prosciutto di San Daniele, from Italy, or Serrano ham from Spain. Use a crisp, French-style baguette (not a sourdough). If the crust of the bread has lost its crispness, toast the baguette in a hot oven for a few minutes, and cool it completely before slicing and smearing it with butter.

1 recipe Scallion Oil (optional)
(see page 19)
1½–2 baguettes, cut into 4
7-inch pieces
1–1½ sticks (4–6 ounces) unsalted
butter, slightly softened
but not greasy
6 ounces prosciutto di Parma,
prosciutto di San Daniele, or Serrano
ham, thinly sliced into about 24 slices

Slice through the center of each piece of baguette horizontally.

TO ASSEMBLE THE SANDWICHES: Smear 2–3 tablespoons of butter over the bottom half of each baguette piece. If you're using scallion oil, spoon 1–2 tablespoons of it over and place about 6 slices of rumpled prosciutto on top. Put the top half of the baguette over the ham, and squeeze the sandwich together with your fingers to compress it before taking the first bite.

Reuben

After tasting the "secret sauce" and creamy coleslaw made by Matt Molina, one of our cooks at Campanile, I knew I had to include in my sandwich book this variation of a Reuben, the king of the deli sandwich board.

Make your Reuben on an authentic Jewish rye bread. And if you're lucky enough to live in L.A., head over to Langer's for the pastrami; or in New York go to Katz's or Pastrami King. Otherwise, find the best hand-cut pastrami in your neighborhood.

TO MAKE THE MAYONNAISE: In the bowl of an electric mixer or in a medium-sized stainless-steel bowl, whisk the egg yolks and salt by hand. Slowly drizzle in the oil, drop by drop, whisking constantly. As the mixture begins to thicken, add a teaspoon of the lemon juice and a teaspoon of water.

Once you've added almost half of the oil, place the bowl in the mixer fitted with a whisk attachment and mix on medium speed, or continue to whisk in the oil by hand. Pour the oil in a slow, steady trickle, scraping down the sides of the bowl as necessary. As the mixture thickens, add a little more of the lemon juice and water, and continue whisking until the remaining oil is completely incorporated and the sauce is thickened.

TO MAKE THE RUSSIAN DRESSING: Place the egg in a small saucepan with water to cover. Bring it to a boil over high heat, then turn the heat down to a low simmer. Simmer the egg 7 minutes, and immediately plunge it into a bowl of ice water to chill. Peel the egg, and separate the yolk from the white. Chop each separately into very small pieces.

In a large bowl, whisk together the mayonnaise, ketchup, Tabasco, Worcestershire sauce, lemon juice, chopped egg, onion, parsley, cornichons, and salt. Adjust the seasonings, to taste.

TO MAKE THE COLESLAW: In a large bowl, combine the mayonnaise, crème fraîche, vinegar or lemon juice, mustard, and Tabasco. Add the sugar,

FOR THE MAYONNAISE

2 extra-large egg yolks

¼ teaspoon kosher salt

1½ cups vegetable oil

2 teaspoons fresh lemon juice

1–2 teaspoons warm water

FOR THE RUSSIAN DRESSING

1 extra-large egg

1 cup mayonnaise (see above)

3 tablespoons ketchup

1 drop Tabasco sauce

⅛ teaspoon Worcestershire sauce

A few drops fresh lemon juice, to taste

2 teaspoons finely chopped red onion

2 teaspoons finely chopped fresh Italian parsley leaves

3 cornichons or gherkins, finely chopped (about 1 tablespoon)

½ teaspoon kosher salt

FOR THE CREAMY COLESLAW

⅓ cup mayonnaise (see above)

3 tablespoons crème fraîche or sour cream

2 tablespoons apple-cider vinegar or lemon juice

1 teaspoon American yellow mustard

2 drops Tabasco sauce

salt, celery seed, and pepper, and stir to combine the ingredients. Add the cabbage, toss to combine, and chill until ready to use.

TO ASSEMBLE THE SANDWICHES: Set half of the bread slices buttered side down, and spread two tablespoons of the Russian dressing to cover. Pile the pastrami over and top with cheese. Place the top slice of bread over the cheese and grill the sandwiches according to the directions on page 8.

Cut the Reubens in half on the diagonal, and serve with a side of creamy coleslaw and any leftover Russian dressing.

¾ teaspoon sugar

½ teaspoon kosher salt

¼ teaspoon celery seed

⅛ teaspoon freshly cracked black pepper

½ head cabbage, shredded to equal 2 cups

8 slices Jewish rye bread

1 pound pastrami, preferably hand-cut

4 ounces Gruyère, sliced into 12–16 ¹⁄₁₆-inch-thick slices

FRIED EGG SANDWICH

You may think that a fried-egg sandwich has to have bacon to taste good. I beg to differ. My Fried Egg Sandwich—slathered with red-pepper saffron mayonnaise, layered with slices of juicy tomato, and piled with crunchy matchstick potatoes—is unbeatable.

Adjust the oven rack to the middle position, and preheat the oven to 350 degrees.

Using a mandoline fitted with the ¼-inch shoelace blade, cut the potatoes into ¼-inch-wide matchsticks. If you don't have a mandoline or it doesn't have a shoelace blade, use a sharp knife to slice the potatoes into ⅛-inch-thick slices, then cut the slices into ¼-inch-wide matchsticks. Soak the potatoes in cold water for about 15 minutes. Drain the water from the potatoes, and pat them dry with a kitchen towel.

Pour the oil into a deep heavy-duty saucepan to fill it halfway. Heat the oil, over medium heat, to 350 degrees, measuring the temperature on a deep-fat-frying thermometer.

Fry the potatoes in 2 or more batches, being careful not to overcrowd them in the pan. Fry them for 2–3 minutes, stirring constantly, until they're lightly browned. Remove them from the oil with a slotted spoon and set on a paper towel to drain. Sprinkle the fried matchsticks generously with salt.

Drizzle a tablespoon of olive oil over the tomato slices, and sprinkle them with salt. Allow them to sit for 5–10 minutes.

Grill the bread according to the directions on page 8.

TO ASSEMBLE THE SANDWICHES: Spoon 1–2 tablespoons of the rouille over half of the bread slices. Pile the lettuce over and place a few slices of tomato on top.

In a 10-inch non-stick skillet, melt 1 tablespoon of the butter over medium-high heat until it starts to bubble. Crack 1 egg into the pan, and stir the yolk a few times to blend it slightly, but not completely, into the white.

1 recipe Rouille (see page 209)
2–4 (about 1 pound) Yukon Gold potatoes, peeled
Vegetable oil, for deep-frying
Kosher salt, to taste

1 tablespoon extra-virgin olive oil, for drizzling over the tomato
1 large ripe tomato, core end discarded, sliced into ¼-inch-thick slices
Kosher salt, to taste

8 slices white or whole-wheat sourdough bread (or see page 219)
1 garlic clove, peeled

½ small head iceberg lettuce, shredded (about 2 cups)

4 extra-large eggs
4 tablespoons unsalted butter
Kosher salt, to taste
Freshly cracked black pepper, to taste

Sprinkle with salt and pepper, and cook for about 45 seconds. Flip the egg over, and cook on the other side for another 45 seconds. Transfer the egg to the sandwich, placing it on the tomato. Pile on the potatoes and cover with the top slice of bread. Cut in half on the diagonal. Wipe out the skillet, and fry the remaining eggs in the same manner.

ODDS & ENDS FOCACCETE

Most of the time, leftover ingredients just don't muster up the same enthusiasm as they did their first time around. But when artfully arranged in little panini rolls, leftovers take on a whole new excitement. These mini-sandwiches are the answer to using up all of those odds and ends you've accumulated after sandwich night at your house. Those few tablespoons of aïoli or pesto, the 6 stray olives, those bits and pieces of roasted red pepper, and that half-ball of mozzarella will no longer hang around in your refrigerator, waiting to be thrown away the following week.

These sandwiches are pretty to look at, easy to put together, and, thank goodness, don't warrant a recipe. Start out with 2½-inch crusty white rolls. To duplicate the flatter, Italian-style *focaccete*, you may have to slice ½ inch or so from the center of your bread. To do this, use a serrated knife to cut the roll in half horizontally, and then trim each half accordingly. Or, if you want to make your own rolls, I've included a recipe for the perfect-size mini-bun (see page 221).

Remember, these are minimal, 5-bite snacks, so stick to simple flavor combinations and don't overstuff them with complicated ingredients. Depending on what you have lying around, you can make one type or an assortment of sandwiches. Just make sure the bread is moistened with a leftover condiment, such as Aïoli (see page 204), Salsa Romesco (page 210), or Basil Pesto (page 212). If you don't have any homemade or store-bought condiments left, improvise by smearing the bread with softened butter or a drizzle of extra-virgin olive oil.

To show off what's inside, layer your ingredients with care and consideration. Rumple a scrap of prosciutto, exposing its curled edge as it leans against the cross-section of a sliced black olive. Combine that remnant of salmon with cucumber slices and hard-cooked egg, stacking the layers unevenly to reveal the colorful fillings. You may want to accent them with a sprig of dill, a fennel frond sprig, or a tiny basil leaf.

Close your eyes. Take a bite. You might just think you're standing at the bar at Café Greco in Rome.

SORT-OF SANDWICHES

Just because the bread isn't on the outside, who says you can't call it a sandwich? Whether layered or skewered, hidden underneath, stacked sideways, or torn into croutons, bread is a component in all of these free-form interpretations. And I call them all sandwiches . . . sort of.

TIAN

With a slice of bread as its base, I turned this classic French gratin into a sort-of sandwich. As the overlapped vegetables bake, their flavors concentrate and the juices are absorbed into the bread. Eaten hot out of the oven or cold the next day (like leftover pizza), this baked sandwich is delicious and satisfying.

TO CARAMELIZE THE ONIONS: In a small skillet, combine 1 tablespoon of the olive oil, the onions, 1 teaspoon of the salt, and $\frac{1}{8}$ teaspoon of the pepper, and sauté over medium-high heat, stirring frequently, for about 10 minutes. When the onions begin to turn color, add a splash or so of water to deglaze the bottom of the pan and prevent them from burning. Continue cooking over medium heat about 45 more minutes, until the onions are very soft and evenly caramelized. Stir in the sherry, and remove from the heat.

TO COOK THE PEPPERS: In a small skillet, combine the peppers, 1 tablespoon of the olive oil, and $\frac{1}{2}$ teaspoon of the salt, and sauté over medium-high heat for about 20 minutes, stirring constantly, until they're soft and tender.

Add the caramelized onions to the peppers, stir in $\frac{1}{8}$ teaspoon of pepper, and remove from the heat.

Adjust the oven rack to the middle position, and preheat the oven to 350 degrees.

Using a mandoline or a sharp knife, slice the zucchini into about 28 $\frac{1}{8}$-inch-thick rounds. Using only the wide end of the squash, cut the crookneck squash in the same manner.

Brush the bottom of a 13-by-9-inch baking dish with a little olive oil. Place the slices of bread close together (it's important that the slices of bread fit snugly in the baking dish in order to cook properly), and evenly distribute the onion-and-pepper mixture over each slice, staying inside of the crust of the bread.

At one end of the bread, place a round of yellow squash over the onion-and-pepper mixture. Place a tomato slice next to the squash, overlapping it

3 tablespoons extra-virgin olive oil

2 medium yellow onions, cut in half through the root and sliced into $\frac{1}{8}$-inch-thick slices

2 teaspoons kosher salt

$\frac{1}{4}$ teaspoon freshly cracked black pepper

1–2 teaspoons water

2 tablespoons dry sherry

2 medium red bell peppers (about 8 ounces each), cut in half lengthwise, seeds, ribs, and stem removed, sliced into long $\frac{1}{8}$-inch-thick slices

Approximately $\frac{1}{2}$ medium green zucchini, $1\frac{1}{2}$ inches in diameter

Approximately $\frac{1}{2}$ medium crookneck yellow squash, $1\frac{1}{2}$ inches in diameter at the wide end

Extra-virgin olive oil, for brushing the pan

4 slices white or whole-wheat sourdough bread (or see page 219)

2 or 3 ripe Romas or other small tomatoes (about $1\frac{1}{2}$ inches in diameter), core end discarded, sliced into $\frac{1}{8}$-inch-thick rounds

1 garlic clove, peeled and finely chopped (about 1 teaspoon)

4 3-inch sprigs fresh thyme leaves

by about an inch. Place a slice of zucchini next to the tomato, overlapping it by an inch. Continue in this manner to make a ring of overlapping vegetables around the bread. (You'll need about 7 slices of each vegetable per slice of bread.) Brush the vegetables with the remaining tablespoon of olive oil. Evenly distribute the garlic and thyme leaves over the vegetables, and sprinkle them with the remaining salt.

Cover the baking dish tightly with plastic wrap and then foil, and bake for 1½ hours. Remove the foil, puncture the plastic to allow the steam to escape, then carefully remove the plastic. Return the dish to the oven, and bake for another 10 minutes, until the vegetables are wrinkled and lightly browned.

PROSCIUTTO AND BLACK PEPPER BISCUIT

Ripping into a salty, chewy loaf of prosciutto and black pepper bread is one of my all-time favorite New York City treats. This traditional Little Italy staple probably started when the butchers offered their prosciutto ends to their favorite neighboring bakeries. The bakers cut the cured-ham scraps into small pieces, tossed them with lots of freshly ground black pepper, and added them to the bread dough. My biscuit, which is made with White Lily, the traditional biscuit flour from the South, is softer and more tender than that East Coast bread, but just as delicious.

Though most of the recipes in this book make four servings, this sort-of sandwich serves five. These biscuits smell so good while baking, you'll need that extra one to ward off your hungry neighbor.

Place the yeast in a small mixing bowl, pour in the buttermilk, and add ¼ cup of the flour. Allow the yeast to soften a few minutes without stirring, then whisk the ingredients together and cover the bowl tightly with plastic wrap. Set aside in a warm place until tiny bubbles appear on the surface, about 30 minutes.

Adjust the oven rack to the middle position, and preheat the oven to 450 degrees.

In the bowl of a food processor fitted with a metal blade, or in the bowl of an electric mixer fitted with the paddle attachment, combine the remaining flour, the salt, baking powder, baking soda, and black pepper, and process on low to incorporate. Add the butter, and pulse on and off a few times, or mix on low, until the mixture is pale yellow and the consistency of fine meal. Transfer it to a large bowl.

Tear 2 ounces of the prosciutto into ½-inch pieces, and roll them into little balls. Toss them with the flour mixture, and make a large well in the

FOR THE BISCUITS

1½ teaspoons (0.2 ounce) packed fresh yeast, or 1 teaspoon active dry yeast
⅓ cup buttermilk
1½ cups White Lily flour, unbleached pastry flour, or unbleached all-purpose flour
¼ teaspoon kosher salt
1 teaspoon baking powder
¼ teaspoon baking soda
1 teaspoon very coarsely cracked fresh black pepper, or 1 teaspoon black peppercorns, very coarsely ground in a mortar and pestle or spice grinder
1 stick (4 ounces) unsalted butter, cut into 1-inch cubes and frozen
3 ounces prosciutto di Parma, prosciutto di San Daniele, or Serrano ham, thinly sliced

FOR DIPPING

¼ cup buttermilk
½ cup (2 ounces) finely grated Parmigiano-Reggiano cheese
Freshly cracked black pepper, to taste

center of it. Pour the yeast mixture into the well, and gently draw in the dry ingredients, mixing until just combined. The dough will be very sticky.

Wash and dry your hands, and dust them with flour. Turn the dough out onto a lightly floured work surface, and gently knead it to gather it into a ball. Pat the dough down flat, to ¾ inch thickness. Dip a 3-inch round biscuit cutter in flour and cut out 4 circles, cutting as closely together as possible and keeping the trimmings intact. As you're cutting, you may need to tuck the prosciutto underneath the biscuit in order to cut all the way through the dough. Press the scraps together to make one more biscuit.

Pour the buttermilk into a shallow bowl, and spread the Parmesan on a small plate. Dip the top of a biscuit into the buttermilk, thoroughly coating it, and then dip it into the cheese. Place the biscuit, cheese side down, on a parchment-lined baking sheet. Continue with the remaining biscuits, placing them 1 inch apart on the baking sheet. Brush the tops with buttermilk. Using your thumb, press a ½-inch impression into the center of the biscuit. Tear the remaining ounce of prosciutto into 5 long strips. Fold the ends of a prosciutto strip into the center, and twist and rumple it into an open flower shape, about 2 inches in diameter. Press the prosciutto into the biscuit, allowing it to cover about three-quarters of the surface. Continue with the remaining prosciutto and biscuits.

Sprinkle the remaining cheese over the tops of the biscuits, and sprinkle with pepper.

Just before baking, turn the oven down to 400 degrees. Bake the biscuits for 20–25 minutes, until they're lightly browned and firm to the touch, rotating the baking sheet halfway through to ensure even baking.

YIELD: 5 biscuits

SORT-OF MUSHROOM SANDWICH

Even though I know you already have your Thanksgiving favorites—those side dishes that you look forward to year after year—this Sort-Of Mushroom Sandwich might just become the new star of your Thanksgiving table. Try it as an alternative to your tired old stuffing alongside Aunt Gerty's yams and marshmallows, and Grandma's green beans with canned fried onions.

½ ounce dried porcini mushrooms

4 slices white or whole-wheat sourdough bread (or see page 219)

3 garlic cloves, peeled

1 large leek, root end trimmed,
dark-green section cut off
and discarded

4 ounces fresh shiitake mushrooms,
wiped clean, stems removed
and discarded

8 ounces Cremini mushrooms, wiped
clean, stems removed and discarded

¼ cup extra-virgin olive oil

1½ teaspoons kosher salt

Freshly cracked black pepper, to taste

2 3-inch sprigs fresh thyme

5 bay leaves

1½ cups chicken stock, homemade
or store-bought low-sodium variety

1½ cups heavy cream

4 extra-large eggs

1–2 tablespoons unsalted butter

In a bowl, combine the dried porcini mushrooms with ½ cup of warm water, and allow them to sit for 30 minutes.

Adjust the oven rack to the middle position, and preheat the oven to 350 degrees.

Place the slices of bread on a baking sheet, and toast them in the oven until lightly browned, about 10–15 minutes. Rub one side of each piece of bread with one of the garlic cloves and finely chop the remaining 2 garlic cloves.

Cut the leek in half lengthwise, and slice it crosswise into ½-inch-thick pieces. Rinse them under cold water, drain, and pat dry with a kitchen towel.

Cut off the tips of the stems of both the shiitake and Cremini mushrooms, and discard. Slice the mushrooms into ⅛-inch-thick slices.

In a large skillet over medium heat, warm 2 tablespoons of the olive oil. Add the leeks, the chopped garlic, salt, and pepper, and cook until the leeks are softened, about 8–10 minutes, being careful not to brown the garlic or leeks. Strain the porcini mushrooms, reserving the soaking liquid. Add all of the mushrooms, the thyme, and one of the bay leaves, and the remaining oil, and cook for another 5–7 minutes, until the mushrooms are soft, stirring occasionally.

Add the chicken stock and the reserved porcini liquid, taking care not to pour any of the grit that may have collected on the bottom. Add the cream and simmer for about 5 minutes to develop the flavor. Season with salt and pepper, to taste. Strain the mixture, reserving the liquid. Remove the bay leaf and thyme sprigs, and discard them.

Crack the eggs into a large mixing bowl, and beat them lightly. Gradually pour the liquid into the eggs, and combine.

Butter the sides and bottom of a 9-by-9-inch baking dish. Place 2 of the slices of bread in the baking dish. (It's important that the slices of bread fit snugly in the baking dish in order to cook properly.) Pour half of the liquid over the bread and allow to sit about 5 minutes, so the bread absorbs the liquid. Spoon the mushroom-leek mixture over the bread, and place the remaining 2 slices of bread over.

Pour the remaining liquid over the bread, and place the bay leaves on the four corners. Cover the baking dish tightly with plastic wrap and then foil, and allow to sit for about 5 minutes to allow the bread to soak up the liquid.

Place the baking dish in a large roasting pan, and fill the roasting pan with 1 inch of water. Transfer to the oven, and bake for 45 minutes. Remove the foil, puncture the plastic to allow the steam to escape, then remove the plastic. Return the dish to the oven for about 10 minutes, until the top of the bread is lightly browned.

Cut into 4 "sandwich" portions and serve.

Skewered Mozzarella

Twelve years ago, as I flipped through Giuliano Bugialli's book, The Foods of Italy, *I noticed a photo of* spiedini di mozzarella. *Right away, I filed it in the "must make one day" section of my brain. I knew that eventually I would find the right time and place for this simple yet delicious-looking appetizer.*

Many years later, Sandwich Night at Campanile proved the perfect venue. Stacked on a rosemary branch and grilled (or baked), the crispy bread and warm, soft mozzarella are drenched with my favorite warm anchovy dressing, bagna cauda. This sort-of sandwich turns into the perfect party food when assembled with extra cheese and bread and passed around on a platter to your guests.

1 recipe Bagna Cauda (see page 18)

½ lemon zested into long strands

8 6-inch straight branches fresh rosemary, or several sprigs fresh rosemary

½ baguette, sliced into ¼-inch-thick slices

1½ pounds (3–4 large balls) fresh mozzarella, sliced into ¼-inch-thick slices

Fresh bay leaves (optional)

Olive oil, for brushing skewers

Kosher salt, to taste

Freshly cracked black pepper, to taste

20 fresh Italian parsley leaves

Add the strands of lemon zest to the bagna cauda and stir to combine.

From each branch, remove most of the rosemary leaves, leaving 1½–2 inches of one end covered in leaves. Place a bread slice on the work surface, and put a piece of mozzarella on it, followed by a fresh bay leaf (optional). Repeat one more time, ending with a slice of bread. You should have a stack that has 3 slices of bread and 2 slices of cheese. Continue with the remaining ingredients, to make 4 stacks total. (If you can't find large rosemary branches, substitute wooden skewers. Soak the wooden skewers in cold water for 20 minutes. As you're assembling, put a few sprigs of fresh rosemary throughout.)

Using the leafless end of a rosemary sprig, skewer one of the stacks through the center, leaving the rosemary leaves exposed on the other end. Turn the stack on its side and, entering from the opposite end, insert another rosemary sprig, leaving the leaves sticking out of the other end. Brush the entire skewer lightly with olive oil, and sprinkle it with a pinch of salt and pepper. Continue in the same manner with the remaining stacks.

TO GRILL: Place the skewers on the hottest part of a charcoal or gas grill and cook for 1–2 minutes, turning frequently, until the cheese just begins to soften and the bread begins to brown.

TO BAKE: Preheat the oven to 400 degrees. Place the skewers on a baking sheet and cook about 5 minutes.

Carefully transfer the skewers to a plate and drizzle with a generous amount of the bagna cauda. Scatter the parsley leaves over.

PANZANELLA

Borrowed from the traditional Tuscan salad, this recipe should be kept under lock and key until summer is in full term and the hot July sun ripens the sweetest, juiciest tomatoes.

Be sure to put a bowl of your favorite extra-virgin olive oil, a bottle of balsamic vinegar, a small ramekin of fleur de sel, and a pepper grinder on the table, so your guests can season this "sandwich" according to their taste.

FOR THE PEPPER MARINADE: On a hot grill, or directly on the stovetop over high heat, char the peppers over an open flame, turning frequently, until the skin is blackened on all sides and the flesh is tender. Place the peppers in a plastic bag, or a bowl covered tightly with plastic wrap, to steam until cool enough to handle. Using a towel, wipe off the charred skin. Tear the peppers into thirds and remove the seeds.

In a small bowl (but one large enough to contain the peppers), put a teaspoon of the olive oil, ½ teaspoon of the balsamic vinegar, 4 or 5 garlic slices, a teaspoon of capers, and ¼ teaspoon chopped anchovy. Stir the ingredients together, and place 1 or 2 basil leaves over to cover. Place one section of a pepper over the leaves. Continue in the same manner—adding marinade ingredients, then the pepper section and basil—for 7 more layers. Allow the peppers to marinate for at least 1 hour or overnight.

FOR THE PEPPER MARINADE

3 medium red bell peppers
(about 8 ounces each)
¼ cup extra-virgin olive oil
2 tablespoons balsamic vinegar
4 garlic cloves, peeled and sliced
into paper-thin slices
2 tablespoons plus 2 teaspoons
capers, perferably salt-packed, rinsed
well, drained, and coarsely chopped
1 or 2 3-inch-long salt-packed
anchovies, rinsed well,
backbone removed, and chopped
(about 1 tablespoon)
9 large or 18 small fresh basil leaves

FOR THE CROUTONS

1 1-pound sourdough white loaf
(or see page 219)
1 tablespoon extra-virgin olive oil
1 garlic clove, peeled

TO PREPARE THE CROUTONS: Adjust the oven rack to the middle position, and preheat the oven to 325 degrees.

Cut the loaf of bread in half and, using your fingers, reach in beneath the crust to pull out 1½–2-inch pieces of the bread. Place the bread chunks on a baking sheet, drizzle them with the olive oil, and toss well. Toast them in the oven for about 15–20 minutes, until they're lightly browned, shaking the pan occasionally to ensure they're evenly baked. When the croutons are cool enough to handle, rub them with the garlic clove and set aside.

In a huge bowl, toss the tomatoes with the salt, oil, half of the parsley, and pepper, to taste. Allow the tomatoes to marinate for 30 minutes.

Remove the red peppers from the marinade, and tear them into long ½-inch-wide strips. Add the peppers and croutons to the tomatoes. Pour the marinade over them, and toss well to combine.

TO SERVE: Transfer half of the panzanella to a platter, distributing the ingredients around evenly. Shave a layer of Parmesan over them, and pile the remaining panzanella over the cheese. Pour any marinade remaining in the bottom of the bowl over the panzanella, drizzle with a little olive oil, and sprinkle with fleur de sel and pepper. Shave a layer of Parmesan over, and scatter the remaining parsley sprigs on top.

FOR THE TOMATOES

3 medium tomatoes, cored
and cut into eighths
½ teaspoon kosher salt
2 tablespoons extra-virgin olive oil
24 small sprigs fresh Italian
parsley leaves
Freshly cracked black pepper, to taste

Approximately ¼-pound wedge
Parmigiano-Reggiano, for shaving
Extra-virgin olive oil, for drizzling
Fleur de sel or kosher salt, to taste
Freshly cracked black pepper, to taste

BUTTERED BREAD WITH SALTY EGGS, BROCCOLINI, AND SLICED CELERY

Rarely is something too salty for me. I just love salt. I might be one of the few diehards who can actually eat the salt-preserved eggs served at the bar at Anissa in New York City. I eat them right out of the shell with a spoon. Alone in my enthusiasm, I wanted to devise a way to get my salt-intolerant friends to join me in my new favorite snack. So this is what I did to cut through some of the salt: I took some bread and smeared it with butter and spooned the egg on top. Not only did my friends become converts, but I was well on my way to my next sort-of sandwich.

This is not a last-minute meal. To preserve the eggs and give them time to gain their rich, salty flavor, you must soak them in a seasoned brine for 6 weeks. Taste the brine before adding the eggs—it should taste saltier than the ocean. After 6 weeks have passed, transfer the eggs to an egg carton and store them in the refrigerator for up to a month. When hard-cooked, the salt-saturated eggs develop a firm, flavorful yolk enveloped in a soft, custardlike white. These are preserved eggs worth waiting for.

There are two ingredients in this sort-of sandwich that you might need to improvise on. Broccolini, sometimes called "asparation," is a hybrid of broccoli and bok choy. If you can't find this pencil-thin version of broccoli (similar in looks to rapini but not bitter at all), use regular broccoli and trim the stalks accordingly. And though a sliced bâtard (or fat baguette) is the perfect size for half of a brined egg to sit upon, you can substitute a slice of sourdough bread cut into thirds or quarters.

By the way, if you ever happen to have a charcoal grill going and a batch of brined eggs sitting in the refrigerator, hard-cook the eggs, slice them in half through the shell, brush them with olive oil, and throw them on the grill, cut side down, for a few minutes. Arrange on a platter and spoon a dollop of Aïoli (see page 204) over the whites of some, and a dollop of Salsa Verde (see page 213) over the others, and you will have a stunning platter of hors d'oeuvres that are delicious and like nothing you've ever tasted before. Remember to serve them with a little spoon for scooping them out of the shell.

TO BRINE THE EGGS: In a small skillet, toast the mustard seeds, fennel seeds, and dill seeds over medium heat for 3–4 minutes, until they begin to release their aromas.

Combine the toasted seeds, bay leaves, black peppercorns, chiles, thyme, and garlic cloves in a 2-quart jar. Place the eggs in the jar one at a time, being careful not to crack any. If you notice that one has cracked, discard it and replace it with another.

In a bowl, whisk the salt into the warm water, and pour the water into the jar. Place a kitchen towel over the eggs to keep them submerged in the salt water, and refrigerate for at least 6 weeks.

FOR THE BRINED EGGS

1 tablespoon yellow mustard seeds

1 tablespoon fennel seeds

1 tablespoon dill seeds

2 bay leaves

1 tablespoon black peppercorns

3 whole dried red chiles

4 3-inch sprigs fresh thyme

3 garlic cloves, peeled

12 extra-large eggs

3 cups kosher salt

8 cups warm water

¼ cup kosher salt

10–12 ounces broccolini or sprouted baby broccoli or broccoli, cut into thin pieces and ends trimmed off

8 ½-inch-thick slices bâtard, or 2 or 3 slices ½-inch-thick white sourdough bread, cut into thirds or quarters

1 garlic clove, peeled

About 10 tablespoons Normandy or imported unsalted butter, slightly softened

8 tiny breakfast radishes, small green stems still attached to half of them

1 head celery, outer stalks peeled, sliced on the extreme diagonal into ¼-inch-thick slices

15 whole celery leaves

1 recipe Bagna Cauda (see page 18)

Carefully remove the eggs, and discard any that have cracked.

In a medium pot, bring 8 cups of water and ¼ cup of salt to a boil. Cook the broccolini for 1–2 minutes in the boiling water, until tender but not soft. It should remain bright green and still be crunchy when you bite into it. Drain, and place it in a large bowl with plenty of ice water to chill for a few minutes. Remove the broccolini from the water, pat it dry with a kitchen towel, and allow it to sit at room temperature.

TO COOK THE EGGS: Bring a medium saucepan of water to a boil. Carefully lower 4 of the eggs into the water, and cook for 6 minutes. Drain, and transfer them to a large bowl of ice water to chill.

Grill the bread according to the directions on page 8. Rub one side of each slice of bread with the garlic clove, and place garlic side up. Allow the bread to cool completely.

Smear one side of each slice of bread with a thick, uneven layer of butter (about 1 tablespoon). Place 2 slices of the bread on each plate.

Using a mandoline or a sharp knife, slice the 4 radishes without the stems into paper-thin slices. Cut the slices into very thin strands lengthwise.

Cut the eggs in half lengthwise through the shell. Using a soupspoon, scoop the egg halves out of the shells, as you would an avocado, and place one half, yolk side up, on each slice of bread.

In a bowl, toss the broccolini, sliced celery, and celery leaves together. Rewarm about 4 tablespoons of the bagna cauda and toss with the broccolini. Pile the vegetables on each plate, next to the egg-topped slices of bread. Place a whole radish (or, if they're large radishes, cut them in half lengthwise) over the broccolini. Scatter a small pinch of the radish strands over the eggs. Drizzle a little bagna cauda around the edges of the broccolini.

FONDUE THE SWISS WAY

Fondue is the ultimate vehicle for a cozy social gathering at home. A French word meaning "melted," fondue is warm cheese at its best, with a dash of white wine, a few spoonfuls of kirsch, and some lemon juice to add an extra punch. Fondue's popularity, confirmed by the vast selection of fondue pots and forks now available in gourmet-cookware shops, is making a comeback since its heyday in the late sixties and early seventies.

For flavor complexity, I use a few different types of assertive, semi-firm cheeses. They should be heated over a very low flame so the cheese melts consistently and doesn't sep-arate into oily puddles and inedible clumps. Earthenware fondue pots are optimal for their even distribution of heat. To dip the chunks of bread, use a long fondue fork and swirl the bread in a figure-eight pattern to coat the bread and prevent the hot mixture from separating. Be forewarned: the first person to lose her bread in the cheese has to kiss everyone at the table. And don't forget the best part of all, la religieuse, *that thin crust of caramelized cheese awaiting you at the bottom of the pot.*

1¼ cups (4 ounces) grated Vacherin Fribourgeois, Fontina Val d'Aosta, or Morbier

1¼ cups (4 ounces) grated cave-aged Gruyère or Beaufort

1¼ cups (4 ounces) grated Appenzeller or Tête de Moine

1 tablespoon potato starch or cornstarch

1 garlic clove, peeled

1 cup dry white wine, such as Chablis or Riesling, to taste

1–2 teaspoons fresh lemon juice

3 tablespoons Kirschwasser or cherry brandy

Freshly cracked black pepper, to taste

1 small white or whole-wheat sour-dough loaf (or see page 219), slightly stale, cut into 1-inch cubes, using as much of the crust as possible

In a large bowl, combine the cheeses with the starch.

Rub the garlic clove on the inside of the earthenware fondue pot, and leave the clove in the pan. Add the wine and lemon juice. Over medium-low heat, bring the liquid to just below a simmer, making sure it doesn't come to a boil.

Add the cheese, one handful at a time, stirring in a figure-eight pattern, waiting for each handful to melt before adding the next. This may take up to 10 minutes. When the mixture is smooth and just begins to bubble, add the kirsch and pepper and simmer another 2–3 minutes, until slightly thickened, stirring constantly.

Set the fondue pot over the warmer and serve with the bread. In order for the cheese to remain smooth, it needs to be kept warm and stirred con-tinuously. If the mixture begins to separate, return the pot to the stove and whisk over medium-low heat until the fondue becomes smooth and creamy.

SORT-OF FRISÉE LARDON

I've taken my favorite bistro salad—frisée, poached egg, and bacon—and turned it into my favorite sort-of sandwich. Large chunks of bacon, rustic hunks of toasted bread, peppery greens, and scoops of soft-cooked egg tossed together with a warm mustard-sherry dressing will satisfy the Francophile in you.

Preheat the oven to 325 degrees.

FOR THE BACON: Cut each strip of bacon into 4 pieces. In a skillet, over medium-low heat, cook the bacon until cooked all the way through but not crisp. Drain it on a paper towel, and reserve the fat.

FOR THE CROUTONS: Cut the loaf of bread in half and reach in beneath the crust to pull out 1½–2-inch pieces of bread. Place the bread chunks on a baking sheet, drizzle them with the olive oil, and toss well. Toast them in the oven for about 15–20 minutes, until they're lightly browned, shaking the pan occasionally to ensure they're evenly baked. When the croutons are cool enough to handle, rub them with the garlic clove and set aside.

TO COOK THE EGGS: Place the eggs in a medium saucepan with water to cover. Bring them to a boil, then turn down the heat to a low simmer. Simmer the eggs for 5 minutes, then plunge them into a large bowl of ice water for a minute or so. Take them out as soon as they're cool enough to handle.

In a huge bowl, toss to combine the radicchio, frisée, dandelion greens, toasted bread, and bacon.

TO MAKE THE VINAIGRETTE: In a medium-sized skillet, over medium heat, warm the bacon fat (and olive oil, if necessary). Add the shallots, and cook them for 2–3 minutes, until they just begin to sizzle. Whisk in the vinegar, salt, and pepper, and cook for about 1 minute. Whisk in the mustard, and cook another 30 seconds. Remove the vinaigrette from the heat, and season with salt and pepper, to taste.

Pour most of the vinaigrette over the salad, and toss well to combine. Cut the top ½ inch off the eggs and, using a spoon, scoop them out of the shells in large spoonfuls into the bowl. Pile the salad onto 4 plates, and drizzle the remaining vinaigrette over each.

6 ounces bacon, preferably applewood-smoked, sliced off the slab into 3 ½-inch-thick strips

FOR THE CROUTONS
1 1-pound white sourdough loaf (or see page 219)
1 teaspoon extra-virgin olive oil
1 garlic clove, peeled

5 extra-large eggs
1 medium head (about 8 ounces) radicchio, leaves removed and torn into large pieces
1 medium head (about 4 ounces) frisée, center core removed, pulled apart into small bunches
1 large bunch (about 4 ounces) dandelion greens, mizuna, or arugula, tough stems removed

FOR THE VINAIGRETTE
½ cup bacon fat (If you don't get enough rendered fat from frying the bacon, add enough olive oil to make up the quantity)
1–2 shallots, peeled and finely chopped (about 2 tablespoons)
¼ cup sherry-wine vinegar
2 teaspoons kosher salt
1 teaspoon freshly cracked black pepper
2 teaspoons Dijon mustard

Fonduta with Truffle Butter

Fonduta, the Italianized version of fondue, is made with white truffles and Fontina Val d'Aosta cheese, and is enriched with egg yolks. Traditionally it's poured over rice, potatoes, or polenta, but my sort-of sandwich serves it in the Swiss style, with bread dipped in. Instead of the hard-to-find and very expensive white truffle, I use the more readily available (and less costly) truffle butter. Porcini butter, found on the same shelf as truffle butter in a well-stocked supermarket, is an alternative to truffle butter for infusing the melted cheese with a deep, earthy flavor.

Keep a watchful eye on the fonduta; if cooked at too high a temperature, the egg yolks will curdle.

9 ounces Fontina Val d'Aosta cheese, cut into ¼-inch pieces

¾ cup whole milk

4 egg yolks, brought to room temperature and beaten

½ cup plus 2 tablespoons truffle butter or porcini butter, softened

½ cup plus 2 tablespoons (2 ounces) aged provolone, grated

1–2 teaspoons fresh lemon juice

1 small white or whole-wheat sourdough loaf (or see page 219), slightly stale, cut into 1-inch cubes, using as much of the crust as possible

Place the Fontina in a heatproof bowl and pour in the milk. Set aside at room temperature to soften, for 2–3 hours.

Bring a pot of water to a gentle simmer. Place the bowl of cheese and milk over the pot (making sure that the bowl isn't touching the water and the flames aren't reaching the bowl), and stir constantly, until the cheese is melted. The mixture may separate as it gets warmer. Remove the bowl from the pot, and let the mixture cool about 5 minutes, stirring occasionally to release the heat.

In a medium bowl, combine the egg yolks and truffle butter. Add them to the cheese mixture, whisking to incorporate them quickly. Put the bowl back over the simmering water, and cook for about 3 minutes, stirring constantly in a figure-eight pattern, until the mixture is thickened, smooth, and velvety. (Keep the heat very low so the mixture doesn't come to a boil.) Gradually add the provolone, stirring constantly. Stir in the lemon juice, to taste.

Transfer to an earthenware fondue pot, set over the warmer, and serve with the cubes of bread. In order for the cheese to remain smooth, it needs to be kept warm and stirred continuously. If the mixture begins to separate, return the pot to the stove and whisk over low heat until the fondue becomes smooth and creamy.

SNACKBREADS

In this sort-of sandwich, the filling is transformed into a topping. Now, don't start getting creative with piles of goopy toppings; the beauty of these bite-size, pizzalike snacks is their minimalist style. Except for a drizzling of olive oil, a pinch of salt, a sprig of herb, and one primary ingredient, such as a scattering of cherry tomatoes, a piece of roasted radicchio, or some braised leeks, these snackbreads are best left plain, simple, and unembellished.

The light, airy texture of these little breads relies on the wet and somewhat messy dough. You'll need to give the dough three rises and three folds to make it manageable to shape. Don't be concerned with perfection when you're shaping; the breads should be intentionally irregular. Start the sponge for the dough around 10 p.m. the night before, so that when the clock strikes "snacktime" on the next day, you're ready to bake. Read through the recipe beforehand and have all of your toppings ready to go. Then, when you assemble the snackbreads, you can move as quickly as possible, making sure the dough doesn't rise too much in the process.

Since I give exact measurements for the toppings for only one snackbread, the total quantities you'll need will depend on how many of each type of snackbread you want to make. Make one or two kinds, or make the entire assortment. Some of the vegetable toppings, such as tomatoes, zucchini, or potatoes, are simply cut and baked with no further preparation to worry about. But others, such as the roasted-radicchio, red-pepper, and braised-leek, require a little bit of preparation ahead of time. Or seek out good-quality commercial toppings, such as roasted red peppers or artichokes, which are available in well-stocked supermarkets.

Prepare the dough according to the instructions on page 219.

Adjust the oven racks to the upper and middle positions, and preheat the oven to 450 degrees.

Line 3 baking sheets with parchment paper, and dust with flour.

Turn the dough out onto a heavily floured work surface. With both hands, gently stretch the dough from underneath until it's about 1 inch thick.

1 recipe dough for Crusty White Loaf
(see page 219)
Flour, for dusting
½ cup extra-virgin olive oil,
for brushing and drizzling
over the toppings

Using a 1½-inch round biscuit or cookie cutter, cut out one circle at a time. (It may be necessary to rotate and twist the cutter as you're cutting through the dough.) Using your hands, stretch each circle of dough from underneath, elongating it into an approximately 2-inch-long oval, and place it on the baking sheet. Working quickly, continue with the remaining circles, spacing them 1½ inches apart on the baking sheet.

Gently, so as not to deflate the dough, and working quickly, so the dough doesn't rise too much, dab the ovals with olive oil, and arrange the toppings on them according to the instructions below. Firmly press the toppings deeply into the dough at irregular intervals with your fingertips, visualizing small valleys and hills you're creating underneath and around the toppings.

Just before baking, toss a few cups of ice into the oven and close the door to create steam.

Bake for about 20 minutes, until lightly browned.

FOR THE CARAMELIZED-ONION-AND-OLIVE SNACKBREAD: Spread the onions unevenly over the dough, leaving a ½-inch border of dough around the edge. Using your fingertips, press and twist the onions into the dough in a random pattern. Press the olives into the dough and sprinkle with cheese.

FOR THE RADICCHIO SNACKBREAD: Twist the wedge of radicchio to spread it out and press it onto the dough. Brush the top with olive oil, and sprinkle it with fleur de sel.

FOR THE LEEK SNACKBREAD: Place the ¼ leek lengthwise over the dough, pressing it in and fanning it out, allowing the ends to drape over the edge. Press the thyme sprigs flat onto the dough, and sprinkle with fleur de sel.

FOR THE ROASTED-RED-PEPPER SNACKBREAD: Rumple the 2 strips of pepper over the snackbread, pressing them into the dough. Press the thyme sprigs flat onto the dough.

FOR THE TOPPINGS

CARAMELIZED ONION AND OLIVE

About 2 tablespoons caramelized onions (see page 113)

2 black olives, such as Kalamata or Nyons, pitted

1 tablespoon finely grated Parmigiano-Reggiano cheese

RADICCHIO

½ wedge Roasted Radicchio (see page 40)

Fleur de sel or kosher salt

LEEK AND THYME

¼ Braised Leek (see page 27)

3 small sprigs fresh thyme

Fleur de sel or kosher salt

ROASTED RED PEPPER

¼ Roasted Red Pepper (see page 143), torn into 2 1-inch-long strips

3 small sprigs fresh thyme

FOR THE ARTICHOKE SNACKBREAD: Cut the artichoke in half or quarters (depending on the size of the artichokes) and place the 2 sections over the dough, facing in opposite directions. Press the thyme sprigs flat onto the dough, and sprinkle with fleur de sel.

FOR THE ZUCCHINI SNACKBREAD: On a mandoline or using a sharp knife, slice the zucchini or squash into paper-thin slices, about $1/8$ inch thick. Arrange the slices in an overlapping row, dab with olive oil, and sprinkle with thyme leaves and fleur de sel.

FOR THE TOMATO SNACKBREAD: Press the tomatoes into the dough in a random pattern. Press the thyme sprigs flat onto the dough, brush with olive oil, and sprinkle with fleur de sel.

FOR THE POTATO-AND-ROSEMARY SNACKBREAD: On a mando-line or using a sharp knife, slice the potato into paper-thin slices, about $1/8$ inch thick. Arrange the slices in an overlapping row and dab with olive oil. Poke the rosemary sprigs into the dough and sprinkle fleur de sel on top.

FOR THE CHAMPAGNE-GRAPE SNACKBREAD: Press the clusters of grapes into the dough, and sprinkle them with the anise or fennel seeds. Poke the rosemary sprigs into the dough, and sprinkle over both sugars.

YIELD: Makes approximately 30 3-by-2-inch oval snackbreads

ARTICHOKE
1 Braised Artichoke (see page 46)
or $1/2$ marinated Roman-style
artichoke
3 small sprigs fresh thyme
Fleur de sel or kosher salt

ZUCCHINI
$1/6$ of a 6-inch zucchini or
crookneck squash
Pinch of fresh thyme leaves
Fleur de sel or kosher salt

TOMATO
6 Sweet 100's, or 3 cherry
tomatoes cut in half
3 small sprigs fresh thyme
Fleur de sel or kosher salt

POTATO AND ROSEMARY
1 small Yukon Gold potato
3 small sprigs fresh rosemary
Fleur de sel or kosher salt

CHAMPAGNE GRAPES
5 tiny clusters of champagne grapes
(with about 5 grapes per cluster)
Pinch of anise seeds or fennel seeds
3 sprigs fresh rosemary
1 teaspoon granulated sugar
Pinch of crystallized sugar
(see sources)

TEA SANDWICHES

Just say the words "tea sandwich" and you immediately think of delicate finger sandwiches filled with cucumber, egg salad, or watercress. Sparse and compact, these small, savory snacks have clung tightly to their Victorian origins: neat, easy to eat, and never so large or filling as to burst the lunching ladies' tight corsets. To this day, few have dared to tamper with this English tradition.

I'm not English and I hate tea. And, quite frankly, I've always found tea sandwiches to be bland and somewhat unsatisfying. Tea sandwiches' ingredients—whether mealy frozen shrimp or wilted watercress—always seem secondary to their presentation. But recently, on a trip to Italy, I reconsidered this English icon.

In a shop tucked between a designer boutique and a fancy lingerie shop in Rome, I encountered the most perfectly coutured stacks of crustless *tremezzini;* they were the most beautiful small, layered sandwiches I had ever seen. Lining the counter of that neighborhood *gastronomia* were dazzling Roman beauties decked out in geometric Pucci-like patterns of colorful, bold fillings. A configuration of roasted red peppers draped around stark white cheese centers were lined up, like models on a runway, along the edge of the bread. Though well designed and carefully arranged, their contents nestled together effortlessly, as if organically composed. Dressed in the finest olive oil, the stacked sandwiches glistened in the shop window, showing off their understated, minimalist interior. Sophisticated and elegant, these were the sandwiches I wanted to make at home.

Leave it to the Italians to make a tea sandwich that actually looks as good as it tastes. Upon seeing these dazzling snacks, I couldn't stop thinking about their endless possibilities.

Keeping in the Italian tradition, I chose simple combinations with concentrated flavors. Whimsical patterns of Gruyère cheese and ham rolled into coils make the prettiest ham-and-cheese sandwich in the world. A repetitive motif of artichoke hearts, hard-cooked egg, and tuna forms an impressive and hearty meal. Fresh mozzarella and herby pesto provide a mellow contrast to prosciutto and black olives. Like the sandwich maker in Rome, I considered color and form as I crafted each one of my own beauties. They don't require long lists of fancy ingredients, but to make these sandwiches look and taste their best, you'll need to shop creatively. Get the counter person at the deli to cut your meat and cheese into paper-thin slices. If you're not baking your own bread, buy a 12-by-3½-inch pullman-style white loaf (a rectangular sandwich loaf) and ask your neighborhood bakery to slice it horizontally into six long slabs. Otherwise, partially freeze the bread and, using a long, serrated knife, carefully cut the loaf into horizontal slabs.

If you're going to go through the trouble of making these, you may as well make more than one type. Each recipe makes three large sandwiches, which get cut into several small, finger-size snacks, but if you want to make less you can cut down the recipe amounts accordingly. When assembling the sandwiches, keep in mind that the front row is the visible, "show-off" row. You don't need to be as fussy with the back half of the sandwich, but remember to fill in the rows from front to back (making sure that the height is consistent), using the scraps of meats, cut-off ends of eggs, and

remnants of roasted peppers when you have them. And always keep any of your leftovers to make Odds & Ends Focaccete (see page 109).

These aren't your everyday lunchbox sandwiches, so give yourself some extra time for assembling them. On the other hand, the fillings require little if any labor at all. Some of the ingredients, such as pesto and marinated artichokes, can be purchased at well-stocked supermarkets. And if you don't have the patience necessary to assemble these the way I do, simply layer the ingredients in a traditional sandwichlike fashion.

After assembling the sandwiches, cover them with a damp towel to keep them from drying out and to conceal the back edge. Stack them on top of each other, or wrap them in a pretty linen towel. Resist cutting them into finger sandwiches until after your guests have had a chance to ooh and aah over them. In their symmetry and simple design, these sandwiches are theatrical snacks that look almost too good to eat.

HAM, GRUYÈRE, AND WHOLE-GRAIN MUSTARD BUTTER

TO MAKE THE MUSTARD BUTTER: In a small bowl, combine the butter, mustard, and salt.

Cut the crusts off the bread and discard them. Cover 4 slices of the bread with a damp towel to keep them from drying out while you're assembling the others.

TO ASSEMBLE THE SANDWICHES: Place the other 2 slices of bread on the counter, with the long edges nearest you. Spread about 2 tablespoons of the mustard butter over each slice, to cover.

Place a slice of ham on top of a slice of cheese and trim to 3½ inches wide by 4–5 inches long (or the same as the width of your bread). (If your ham and cheese slices are too small, overlap another slice of each to make up the difference.) Repeat to create 7 more stacks.

Beginning with the shorter end of one of the stacks, roll it up halfway (leaving a flat, unrolled section about 2 inches wide). Place the roll on the left end of one of the slices of bread, with the coiled section closer to the center, and the edges of the flat section draping slightly over the edge of the bread. Repeat with one more stack, and place it on the right end in the same manner.

Roll up the remaining stacks completely, placing the coils seam side down on the bread after you've rolled each one, aligning them with the front edge. Don't worry if the ham and cheese hang over the back edge; it won't be seen.

Place the top slice of bread over the rolls, and cover the sandwich with a damp towel to keep it from drying out. Assemble the others in the same manner.

Before serving, cut each large sandwich into 10 slices. (Each end of each large sandwich, though it doesn't have a roll of ham and cheese, is still a sandwich.)

YIELD: 30 sandwiches

FOR THE MUSTARD BUTTER
1 stick (4 ounces) unsalted butter, softened
¼ cup whole-grain mustard
¼ teaspoon kosher salt

1 Tea Sandwich Loaf (see page 222), or 1 12-by-3½-inch pullman-style white loaf, sliced horizontally into 6 long slabs

1½ pounds Gruyère cheese, sliced into 30 ⅟16-inch-thick slices
1½ pounds smoked ham, such as Black Forest, sliced into 12–16 ⅟16-inch-thick slices

Mozzarella, Prosciutto, and Olive

Cut or tear 2 or 3 slices of the prosciutto into several 1-inch-wide strips. Wrap half of the olives in thin strips of prosciutto. Cut off one of the pointed ends of the wrapped olives, crosswise, to create a flat front.

Slice the mozzarella balls into ½-inch-thick slices, and cut each slice into quarters.

Cut the crusts off the bread and discard them. Cover 4 slices of the bread with a damp towel to keep them from drying out while you're assembling the others.

TO ASSEMBLE THE SANDWICHES: Place the other 2 slices of bread on the counter with the long edges nearest you, and spread about 2 heaping tablespoons of pesto over each slice, to cover.

Trim off one of the longer edges of the remaining prosciutto slices to make a straight edge on one side.

Place a prosciutto-wrapped olive on the front left corner of one of the slices of bread, aligning the cut side of the olive with the front edge of the bread. Place a mozzarella quarter with the flat edge aligned with front edge of bread, leaning against the olive. Pick up a piece of the prosciutto and, aligning the straight-cut edge with the front edge of bread, drape it over the mozzarella, tucking the left end of the prosciutto underneath the left side of the olive, allowing the rest of the prosciutto slice to lie on the bread. Lay another prosciutto-wrapped olive on top of the prosciutto resting on the bread, and nestle it against the mozzarella. Lift up the rest of the prosciutto slice (you may need to use another piece of prosciutto at this point to achieve the weaving effect), and place another quarter of mozzarella underneath it, aligning the cut edges with the front edge of the bread, as before. Repeat this process of weaving the prosciutto under the olives and over the mozzarella wedges, working your way across the front edge of the bread. You'll probably need about 3 or 4 slices of prosciutto for this process. Place 2 layers of prosciutto slices to cover the remaining surface of bread behind the

6 ounces prosciutto di Parma, prosciutto di San Daniele, or Serrano ham thinly sliced into about 24 slices
8 ounces black olives, such as Kalamata or Nyons (about 48), pitted
2½ pounds (4–5 large balls) fresh mozzarella
1 Tea Sandwich Loaf (see page 222), or 1 12-by-3½-inch pullman-style white loaf, sliced horizontally into 6 long slabs
1 recipe Basil Pesto (see page 212)

front woven row. Continue to make rows of olives (using the cut-off pointed ends) and rows of mozzarella on top of the prosciutto, making sure that it's the same height as the front.

Place the top slice of bread over, pressing gently to even the surface of the sandwich. Cover with a damp towel to keep it from drying out. Assemble the other 2 sandwiches in the same manner.

Before serving, cut each large sandwich into 8 sections, making the cuts after each row of mozzarella.

YIELD: 24 sandwiches

ROASTED RED PEPPER, GOAT CHEESE, AND BASIL

On a hot grill, or directly on the stovetop over high heat, char the peppers over an open flame, turning frequently until the skin is blackened on all sides and the flesh is tender. Place them in a plastic bag or in a bowl covered tightly with plastic wrap to steam until cool enough to handle. Using a towel, wipe off the charred skin. Remove the seeds and ribs, keeping the peppers intact.

TO MAKE THE VINAIGRETTE: In a medium bowl, whisk to combine the shallot, vinegar, olive oil, rosemary, salt, and pepper, to taste. Place the mixture in a shallow container, and add the roasted peppers, tossing to coat. Marinate the peppers at least 2 hours or overnight.

TO MAKE THE GOAT-CHEESE MIXTURE: In a large bowl, combine the goat cheese, cream, walnut oil, and salt, to taste. Cover with plastic wrap, and chill for about 1 hour, until firm.

Roll the goat-cheese mixture into 33 logs, 4–5 inches long and ½ inch wide (or the same width as your bread), setting the remaining mixture aside. Freeze logs for about 10 minutes, until firm.

TO ASSEMBLE THE SANDWICH: Cut the crusts off the bread and

Approximately 9 medium peppers (about 8 ounces each), or 3 8-ounce jars or cans of commercial roasted red peppers

FOR THE VINAIGRETTE

1 shallot, peeled and finely chopped

½ cup balsamic vinegar

1½ cups extra-virgin olive oil

1 tablespoon finely chopped fresh rosemary

½ teaspoon kosher salt

2 teaspoons freshly cracked black pepper

discard them. Cover the bread slices with a damp towel to keep them from drying out while you're assembling the others.

Place 2 slices of bread on the counter with the long edges nearest you. Brush each slice lightly with the vinaigrette that the peppers were marinating in.

Cut the peppers into triangular thirds with bases approximately 4 inches wide. (Some peppers will yield more than 3 triangles; you should have 33 total.) Place a pepper slice on the counter, interior side face-up and the wider base of the slice nearest you. Place a basil leaf across the lower section. Remove 11 of the goat-cheese logs from the freezer. Place one of the logs lengthwise over the basil leaf and pepper. Starting at the bottom of the triangle, roll the pepper around the goat-cheese log to enclose it. Slice off one end of the roll, to expose the goat cheese and basil, and reserve the trimmings. (If your goat cheese is too soft, you may need to freeze it longer to make it easier to get a clean slice.)

Place a pepper roll on the left edge of one of the slices of bread, seam side down and cut side aligned with the front edge of the bread. Continue making logs and placing them on the bread seam side down after you've rolled each one.

If necessary, spread a thin layer of goat cheese along the back edge of the bread slice, where the pepper rolls didn't reach, and arrange the reserved pepper trimmings along the back edge, making sure that it's the same height as the front.

Place the top slice of bread over the pepper rolls, and cover with a damp towel to keep from drying out. Assemble the other 2 sandwiches in the same manner.

Before serving, cut each large sandwich into 11 sections, slicing in between the rolled peppers.

YIELD: 33 sandwiches

FOR THE GOAT CHEESE
MIXTURE
2 cups fresh goat cheese
¼ cup heavy cream
¼ cup walnut oil or olive oil
1 teaspoon kosher salt

33 large basil leaves

1 Tea Sandwich Loaf (see page 222),
or 1 12-by-3½-inch walnut loaf or
whole-wheat sandwich loaf, sliced
horizontally into 6 long slabs

Smoked Salmon, Cucumber, and Dill Crème Fraîche

TO HARD-COOK THE EGGS: Place the eggs in a small saucepan with water to cover. Bring to a boil over high heat, then turn the heat down to a low simmer. Simmer the eggs for 7 minutes, and immediately plunge them into a large bowl of ice water to chill. Peel the eggs, and cut ½ inch off the pointed end, to expose the yolk slightly. Using an egg slicer or a sharp knife, slice the eggs lengthwise into thin slices.

Stack a few slices of cucumber on top of one another, and cut off about ¼ inch from one of the sides of the stack to create a flat edge. Continue with the remaining cucumber slices.

TO MAKE THE DILL CRÈME FRAÎCHE: In a medium bowl, whisk to combine the crème fraîche, shallot, and chopped dill. Add the lemon juice and salt, to taste.

Cut the crusts off the bread and discard them. Cover 4 slices of the bread with a damp towel to keep them from drying out while you're assembling the others.

TO ASSEMBLE THE SANDWICH: Place the other 2 slices of bread on the counter with the long edges nearest you, and spread about 2–3 tablespoons of the dill crème fraîche over each slice, to cover. Scatter about 15 dill sprigs over one of the slices of bread, allowing some of the sprigs to hang over the front edge slightly.

Place one piece of the salmon on the left edge of the bread, slightly folded over onto itself to give it height. (If the piece of salmon doesn't reach the back edge of the bread, add another small piece.) To the right of the salmon, place a slice of cucumber, leaning it against the salmon on a diagonal and aligning the cut edge of the cucumber slice with the front edge of the bread. Place a slice of egg over the cucumber, aligning the cut edges of the egg and cucumber. Place another slice of cucumber on top of the egg. Place a piece of salmon, slightly folded over onto itself, next to the cucumber, and

4 extra-large eggs

1 or 2 Japanese, Persian, or English cucumbers, unpeeled, cut horizontally into ⅛-inch-thick slices

FOR THE DILL CRÈME FRAÎCHE
1 cup crème fraîche or sour cream
1 shallot, peeled and finely chopped (about 2 tablespoons)
1 tablespoon finely chopped fresh dill leaves, plus about 45 small sprigs
2–3 teaspoons fresh lemon juice
1 teaspoon kosher salt

1 Brioche Loaf (see page 217), or 1 Tea Sandwich Loaf (see page 222), or 1 12-by-3½-inch pullman-style white or brioche loaf, sliced horizontally into 6 long slabs

9½ ounces smoked salmon or gravlax, thinly sliced and cut into strips about 1½ inches wide and 5–6 inches long

continue across the front edge with the egg, cucumber, and salmon. Complete the sandwich by continuing the rows of salmon, cucumber, and egg to the back edge, making sure it's all the same height, from front to back.

Place the top slice of bread over the rows, and cover it with a damp towel to keep it from drying out. Assemble the other 2 sandwiches in the same manner.

Before serving, cut each large sandwich into 8 pieces, making the cuts after each row of cucumbers.

YIELD: 24 sandwiches

Tuna, Artichoke, and Hard-Cooked Egg

TO HARD-COOK THE EGGS: Place the eggs in a small saucepan with water to cover. Bring to a boil over high heat, then turn the heat down to a low simmer. Simmer the eggs for 7 minutes, and immediately plunge them into a large bowl of ice water to chill. Peel the eggs, and cut a ½ inch off the pointed end, to expose the yolk slightly. Cut them into quarters.

Cut the artichoke hearts in half lengthwise.

Cut the crusts off the bread and discard them. Cover 4 slices of the bread with a damp towel to keep them from drying out while you're assembling the others.

TO ASSEMBLE THE SANDWICH: Place the other 2 slices of bread on the counter with the long edges nearest you. Spread about 2 tablespoons of the aïoli over each slice, to cover.

Place an egg quarter on each corner of one of the slices of bread, with the rounded side facing outward, exposing the center cross-section of the egg along the front edge of the bread. Place another egg quarter behind it, to make a row of eggs.

4 extra-large eggs

2 recipes Braised Artichokes (see page 46) or 8 marinated Roman-style artichokes

1 Tea Sandwich Loaf (see page 222) or Brioche Loaf (see page 217), or 1 12-by-3½-inch pullman-style white loaf, sliced horizontally into 6 long slabs

1 recipe Aïoli or Lemon Aïoli (see page 204), made with the olive oil from the braised artichokes

12 ounces tuna in olive oil, preferably Italian or Spanish

Place chunks of tuna next to the egg, creating a row from the front to the back edge. Fan out an artichoke heart slightly and place it next to a row of tuna, with the stem facing toward the back edge of the bread and the interior of the heart along the front edge. Make another row of egg quarters in the same manner as the first, followed by a row of tuna and a row of artichoke heart, continuing in this manner until you've worked your way across the entire slice of bread. Fill in the back edge with artichoke scraps.

Place the top slice of bread over the rows and cover it with a damp towel to keep it from drying out. Assemble the other 2 sandwiches in the same manner.

Before serving, cut each large sandwich into 6 pieces, making the cut after each row of tuna.

YIELD: 18 sandwiches

SANDWICH CAKES AND COOKIES

When I decided to write a sandwich book, I thought to myself: Finally, an uncomplicated volume with no technical baking recipes or long-winded instructions. This book would be all savory foods, without a single teaspoonful of sugar and not a mention of creaming butter. But, eventually, my true nature got the best of me, and before I knew it, there was an entire chapter dedicated to sweets. And not just to any sweets, but to sandwiched sweets.

There are no complicated techniques or fancy equipment required to make these desserts. You will have to dig into the sugar canister, but you won't have to turn your savory kitchen into a pastry kitchen.

CARROT CAKE
CLUB SANDWICH

Like its savory counterpart, this dessert "club" has three layers.

Adjust the oven rack to the middle position, and preheat the oven to 325 degrees.

Spread the walnuts on a baking sheet and toast them in the oven for about 10–12 minutes, until lightly browned.

Brush the melted butter over the bottom and sides of an 11-by-16-inch baking sheet with 1-inch-high sides. Place a sheet of parchment paper on the bottom of the pan, smoothing it out with the palm of your hand to remove the wrinkles. Brush another light coat of the melted butter over the paper.

Turn the oven up to 350 degrees.

Over a large bowl, sift the flour, baking powder, baking soda, cinnamon, salt, nutmeg, ground ginger, allspice, and cloves together.

TO MAKE THE CAKE: In the bowl of an electric mixer fitted with the whisk attachment, whip the brown sugar and eggs on medium-high speed for 10 minutes, until the eggs have lightened in color.

Add the vanilla extract and grated ginger, and mix on medium to combine.

Add the dry ingredients and the oil alternately, in 3 batches, mixing on low until just combined.

Fold in the carrots, pineapple, walnuts, and raisins.

Pour the mixture into the prepared baking sheet, and spread it out evenly. Bake the cake for about 25 minutes, until it's lightly browned and springy to the touch. Allow to cool.

If you're not assembling the cakes that day, cover the baking sheet tightly with plastic wrap, and refrigerate (the cake can be prepared up to 2 days in advance). Bring the cake up to room temperature before frosting.

If the cake has risen unevenly, carefully slice off the higher areas with a

½ cup coarsely chopped walnuts

2 tablespoons unsalted butter, melted, for brushing the pan

FOR THE CAKE

1½ cups unbleached pastry flour or unbleached all-purpose flour

1¾ teaspoons baking powder

1¼ teaspoons baking soda

1¾ teaspoons ground cinnamon

1 teaspoon kosher salt

¼ teaspoon freshly grated nutmeg

½ teaspoon ground ginger

Scant ½ teaspoon ground allspice

Pinch of ground cloves

1½ cups light-brown sugar

3 extra-large eggs

1 tablespoon pure vanilla extract

2¼ teaspoons grated fresh ginger

¾ cup plus 1 tablespoon vegetable oil

2½ cups peeled grated carrots

¼ cup crushed pineapple, well drained

½ cup golden raisins, chopped

FOR THE FROSTING

14 ounces cream cheese, softened

1 stick (4 ounces) unsalted butter

¾ cup powdered sugar, sifted

¼ cup crème fraîche or sour cream

serrated knife. Using a 3-inch round cookie or biscuit cutter, cut out 18 circles as closely together as possible.

TO MAKE THE FROSTING: In the bowl of an electric mixer fitted with the paddle attachment, cream the cream cheese, butter, and powdered sugar on high speed for about 3 minutes. Using a rubber spatula, scrape down the sides of the bowl, and mix for another 2 minutes, until the frosting is light and fluffy.

Add the crème fraîche and mix until just combined. (The frosting can be made up to 2 days in advance and stored, covered, in the refrigerator.)

TO FROST THE CAKES: Using a metal spatula or a pastry bag fitted with a #3 plain tip, spread or pipe a ¼-inch-thick layer of frosting over the top surface of all of the cake circles. Aligning the edges, place one circle on top of another to make 6 3-layer cakes.

Turn a 1-cup measuring cup (or something of similar size) upside down, and place one of the cakes on it. The edges of the cake should hang over the edges of the cup slightly. If you're using a pastry bag, pipe vertical rows of frosting down the sides of the cake, smooth them out with a spatula. Otherwise, use a spatula to spread the frosting on the sides. Using a spoon or spatula, make small peaks in the frosting on the top of the cake. Frost the remaining cakes in the same manner.

YIELD: 6 mini–layer cakes

CHOCOLATE CAKE CLUB SANDWICH

This all-American devil's-food recipe makes six mini-cakes that are rich and moist and pretty to look at. When buying your cocoa powder and chocolate, try to find Scharffen Berger, Valrhona, or Chocolates El Rey.

TO MAKE THE CAKE BATTER: Adjust the oven rack to the middle position, and preheat the oven to 350 degrees.

Brush the melted butter over the bottom and sides of an 11-by-16-inch baking sheet with 1-inch-high sides. Place a sheet of parchment paper on the bottom of the pan, smoothing it out with the palm of your hand to remove the wrinkles. Brush another light coat of the melted butter over the paper.

In a small saucepan over medium heat, whisk together the water and cocoa powder. Bring to a boil, whisking constantly to dissolve the cocoa powder. Remove the pan from the heat, and whisk in the chocolate, vanilla extract, and butter. Stir in the crème fraîche, and transfer to a large mixing bowl.

In the bowl of an electric mixer fitted with the whisk attachment, whip the eggs and yolks and sugar on medium-high for 5–8 minutes, until they become thick and mousselike.

Over a bowl, sift the flour, baking soda, baking powder, and salt to combine and set aside.

Slowly add the eggs and sugar to the chocolate mixture, whisking to combine them. Gently fold in the flour mixture in 3 batches to incorporate, deflating the batter as little as possible.

Pour the batter into the baking sheet, and spread it out evenly. Bake the cake for 18–20 minutes, until a toothpick inserted in the center comes out clean and the cake is springy to the touch. Allow to cool.

If you're not assembling the cakes that day, cover the baking sheet tightly with plastic wrap and refrigerate (the cake can be prepared 2 days in advance). Bring the cake up to room temperature before frosting it.

2 tablespoons unsalted butter, melted, for brushing the pan

FOR THE CAKE

1 cup water

½ cup unsweetened cocoa powder

6 ounces bittersweet chocolate, melted

1 tablespoon plus 1 teaspoon pure vanilla extract

1½ sticks (6 ounces) unsalted butter, softened

½ cup plus 6 tablespoons crème fraîche or sour cream

4 extra-large eggs

2 extra-large egg yolks

1½ cups granulated sugar

2½ cups plus 2 tablespoons unbleached all-purpose flour

1 tablespoon baking soda

2 teaspoons baking powder

1 teaspoon kosher salt

FOR THE FROSTING

½ cup plus 1 tablespoon unsweetened cocoa powder, plus extra for dusting over the top of the cake

½ cup plus 1 tablespoon water

3 tablespoons corn syrup

12 ounces bittersweet chocolate, melted

TO MAKE THE FROSTING: In a small saucepan, whisk together the cocoa, water, and corn syrup. Place the pan over medium heat, and bring the mixture to a simmer, whisking constantly, until it's smooth and thickened. Remove it from the heat, and whisk in the chocolate and cognac. Cool completely.

In the bowl of an electric mixer fitted with the whisk attachment, cream the butter on medium-high speed for about 3–5 minutes, until it lightens in color. Add the powdered sugar, scraping down the sides of the bowl as necessary.

Stir in the melted-chocolate mixture by hand. Let the frosting sit in a cool place or refrigerate until it becomes stiff enough to spread, no longer than 30 minutes.

TO FROST THE CAKES: If the cake has risen unevenly, carefully slice off the higher areas with a serrated knife. Using a 3-inch round cookie or biscuit cutter, cut out 18 circles as closely together as possible. Using a metal spatula or a pastry bag fitted with a #3 plain tip, spread or pipe a ¼-inch-thick layer of frosting over the top surface of all the circles. Aligning the edges, place one circle on top of another to make 6 3-layer cakes.

Turn a 1-cup measuring cup (or something of similar size) upside down, and place one of the cakes on it. If you're using a pastry bag, pipe vertical rows of frosting down the sides of the cake, smooth them out with a spatula. Otherwise, use a spatula to spread the frosting on the sides. Using a spoon or spatula, make small peaks in the frosting on the top of the cake. Frost the remaining cakes in the same manner. Sift a fine layer of cocoa powder over the top of each.

YIELD: 6 mini–layer cakes

2 tablespoons cognac

1½ sticks (6 ounces) unsalted butter

½ cup plus 3 tablespoons powdered sugar

BLUM'S SANDWICH CAKE

A few years ago, Nora Ephron asked my friend Margy Rochlin to ask me if I would be willing to give her a recipe for strawberry ambrosia. In exchange, she would send her coveted recipe for Blum's coffee-crunch cake. How could I say no to that offer? I had been dreaming about that angel-food-and-whipped-cream dessert since the late sixties, when Blum's Coffee Shop in Beverly Hills closed. There was just one small problem: I had never made an ambrosia.

Nora kept up her end of the bargain; she was probably too busy writing and directing movies to realize that I didn't keep up mine. Now that the whole world has my version of your Blum's cake, Nora, I promise I'll get cracking on that ambrosia.

By making individual cakes, you can tailor the sweetness by adding more or less of the honeycomb and hot fudge. If you have either of them left over, cover them well and refrigerate them to serve with ice cream another time.

TO MAKE THE CAKE BATTER: Adjust the oven rack to the middle position, and preheat the oven to 350 degrees.

Brush the melted butter over the bottom and sides of an 11-by-16-inch baking sheet with 1-inch high sides. Place a sheet of parchment paper on the bottom, and smooth it out with the palm of your hand to remove the wrinkles. Brush another light coat of the melted butter over the paper.

Using a fine-mesh sieve, sift 1 cup of the sugar 2 times and set aside. Combine the remaining ¼ cup of the sugar with the flour and salt, and sift them together 3 times.

In the bowl of an electric mixer fitted with the whisk attachment, whip the egg whites and the lemon juice on medium speed until foamy, about 2–3 minutes. Add the cream of tartar, and whip until the whites form very soft peaks, about 3–4 minutes. Very gradually, add the 1 cup of sifted sugar, and whip until the whites reach medium-soft peaks, become shiny, and no longer feel gritty when you rub them between your fingers. Add the vanilla extract, and mix to combine.

Remove the bowl from the mixer, and gently fold in the flour mixture in

2 tablespoons unsalted butter, melted, for brushing on the baking sheet

FOR THE ANGEL FOOD CAKE
1¼ cups sugar
1 cup unbleached pastry flour or unbleached all-purpose flour
½ teaspoon kosher salt
10 extra-large egg whites
1 teaspoon fresh lemon juice
1 teaspoon cream of tartar
1 teaspoon pure vanilla extract

FOR THE HOT FUDGE
½ cup plus 2½ tablespoons water
½ cup light corn syrup
¼ cup sugar
½ cup plus 3 tablespoons cocoa powder
7½ ounces bittersweet chocolate, melted
¼ cup brandy or cognac
¼ cup brewed coffee

FOR THE HONEYCOMB
¼ cup water
1½ cups sugar
¼ cup light corn syrup
1 tablespoon baking soda, sifted

3 batches, incorporating it thoroughly while deflating the batter as little as possible.

Pour the batter into the prepared baking sheet and spread it evenly. Bake for 12–15 minutes, until the cake is lightly browned and springy to the touch. Allow to cool in the pan.

If you're not assembling the cakes that day, cover the baking sheet tightly with plastic wrap and leave at room temperature (the cake can be prepared 1 day in advance).

TO MAKE THE HOT FUDGE SAUCE: In a large saucepan, over medium heat, combine the water, corn syrup, sugar, and cocoa powder. Bring to a boil, stirring constantly. Remove from the heat, whisk in the chocolate, cognac, and coffee, and set aside to cool. The hot fudge can be stored indefinitely in the refrigerator.

TO MAKE THE HONEYCOMB: In a medium-sized deep heavy-duty saucepan, stir the water, sugar, and corn syrup together. Clip a candy thermometer onto the inside of the pan. Over medium-high heat, bring the mixture to a boil without stirring. Using a pastry brush dipped in water, brush down the sides of the pan to remove any undissolved sugar granules. Continue cooking until the sugar reaches 300 degrees on the candy thermometer (hard-crack stage), then remove from the heat. The mixture should be a very pale straw color.

Working quickly, add the baking soda all at once to the sugar mixture, and whisk for a few seconds, until the baking soda is incorporated. The liquid will bubble up and become foamy. In one smooth movement, pour it onto a non-stick baking mat or a parchment-lined baking sheet. It will spread out, puff up slightly, and have a slightly porous, shiny surface. Allow it to harden for about 20 minutes, without touching or moving it. Cut the honeycomb into uneven ½-inch pieces. If you're not using the honeycomb that day, store it in an airtight container at room temperature. The honeycomb will last 1–2 days before it begins to lose its crunch.

TO MAKE THE WHIPPED CREAM: In the bowl of an electric mixer fitted with the whisk attachment, whip the cream and crème fraîche on low speed until the cream thickens enough not to spatter. Increase the speed to

FOR THE WHIPPED CREAM
1¼ cups heavy cream
¼ cup plus 1 tablespoon crème fraîche or sour cream

medium-high, and continue to whip until the cream just begins to hold soft peaks.

If the cake has risen unevenly, carefully slice off the higher areas with a serrated knife. Using a 3-inch round cutter, cut out 12 circles as closely together as possible. Place half of the circles on serving plates.

TO ASSEMBLE THE CAKES: Spoon just enough whipped cream over the top of each circle to cover it. Spoon a little hot fudge over the cream, allowing it to run down the sides of the cake. Scatter about 5 or 6 pieces of the broken honeycomb on top of each cake. Place another circle of cake on top, aligning the edges with the bottom circle and pressing down gently to help it adhere. Top the cake with crème fraîche, hot fudge, and honeycomb. Scatter a few more pieces of honeycomb around the plate before serving. Continue in the same manner with the remaining cakes.

YIELD: 6 2-layer cakes

LEMON CAKE CLUB
SANDWICH IN A GLASS

The beauty of this cake, presented in a see-through glass, is that the colorful layers of berries, sauce, and lemon cream aren't hidden behind a layer of icing. You'll have to eat this tart and saucy dessert, somewhere between a trifle and a layered parfait, with a spoon.

It's a lot easier to construct a three-layer cake when you have the support of a glass. At the restaurant, we make these club cakes in a "rocks" glass that is 2¾ inches in diameter and about 3½ inches tall. You'll need to cut your cake circles out slightly smaller than the diameter of the glass you're using, so they fit inside snugly.

TO MAKE THE LEMON CREAM: In a medium stainless-steel or other non-reactive heatproof bowl, whisk together the lemon juice, lemon zest, lime juice, lime zest, eggs, egg yolks, and sugar.

Bring a pot of water to a gentle simmer. Place the bowl over the pot, making sure that the bowl isn't touching the water. Rotate the bowl from time to time, and stir the mixture occasionally. Cook it for about 25 minutes, until it's very thick.

Using a fine-mesh sieve, strain the lemon curd and cool to room temperature.

Transfer the mixture to a blender or a food processor fitted with a metal blade. Add the butter, 2 tablespoons at a time, mixing for a few seconds after each addition, just long enough to incorporate the butter. Chill the lemon cream for 30 minutes to an hour or up to 2 days.

Adjust the oven rack to the center position, and preheat the oven to 325 degrees.

Spread the almonds on a baking sheet, and toast them in the oven for about 3–5 minutes, until they're lightly browned.

TO MAKE THE CAKE: Turn the oven up to 350 degrees.

Brush some of the melted butter over the bottom and sides of an

FOR THE LEMON CREAM

½ cup fresh lemon juice
(about 3 or 4 lemons)

2 tablespoons finely chopped
lemon zest

½ cup fresh lime juice
(about 5 or 6 limes)

2 tablespoons finely chopped
lime zest

3 extra-large eggs

3 extra-large egg yolks

¾ cup granulated sugar

1 stick (4 ounces) unsalted butter,
slightly softened

¼ cup sliced almonds

2 tablespoons unsalted butter,
melted, for brushing the pan

FOR THE CAKE

2 cups unbleached all-purpose
flour, sifted

1 teaspoon baking powder

⅛ teaspoon kosher salt

8 extra-large eggs, separated

2 cups granulated sugar

¼ cup fresh lemon juice
(about 2 lemons)

2 teaspoons finely chopped
lemon zest

11-by-16-inch baking sheet with 1-inch-high sides. Place a sheet of parchment paper on the bottom of the pan, smoothing it out with the palm of your hand to remove the wrinkles. Brush another light coat of the melted butter over the paper.

Over a bowl, sift to combine the flour, baking powder, and salt.

In the bowl of an electric mixer fitted with the whisk attachment, beat the egg yolks and 1 cup of sugar on medium-high speed for about 5 minutes, until the mixture forms a ribbon when you lift the whisk away from it. Add the lemon juice and zest, and mix to combine them with the egg yolks. Transfer to a large mixing bowl.

Fold in the flour mixture, ¼ cup at a time.

In the bowl of a clean and dry mixer fitted with the whisk attachment, whisk the egg whites on low speed, until they form soft peaks. Turn the mixer to high and gradually add the remaining sugar, whisking until the whites form stiff peaks. Fold the whites into the batter.

Pour the batter into the baking sheet, spreading it evenly. Bake the cake for 25–30 minutes, until a toothpick inserted in the center comes out clean. Allow it to cool slightly.

If you're not assembling the cakes that day, cover the baking sheet tightly with plastic wrap, and refrigerate (the cake can be prepared up to 2 days in advance).

TO MAKE THE STRAWBERRY SAUCE: In a food processor fitted with a metal blade, purée the berries (with the juice if you're using frozen ones) and sugar until smooth, being careful not to overprocess them.

TO MAKE THE BOYSENBERRY SAUCE: In a food processor fitted with a metal blade, purée the berries (with the juice if you're using frozen ones) and sugar. Strain the purée through a fine-mesh sieve and discard the seeds.

TO MAKE THE WHIPPED CREAM: In the bowl of an electric mixer fitted with a whisk attachment, whip the heavy cream and crème fraîche on medium-low speed until thickened. Increase the speed to medium-high, and continue to whip until the cream holds soft peaks. Measure out a heaping ½ cup of the cream into a small bowl, and chill. Fold the remaining whipped cream into the lemon mixture.

FOR THE STRAWBERRY SAUCE
2 cups fresh strawberries, stems removed, or unsweetened frozen ones, thawed, with their juice
1–2 tablespoons granulated sugar

FOR THE BOYSENBERRY SAUCE
2 cups fresh boysenberries or unsweetened frozen ones, thawed, with their juice
6 tablespoons granulated sugar

¾ cup heavy cream
3 tablespoons crème fraîche or sour cream

FOR THE LAYERS
1 pint fresh strawberries, hulled, cut in half
1 pint fresh blueberries
1 pint fresh boysenberries

¼ cup powdered sugar, for dusting over the top

TO ASSEMBLE THE CLUB CAKES: Using a round cookie or biscuit cutter just slightly smaller than the diameter of the glasses you're using (see headnote), cut out 15 circles as closely together as possible. Using a serrated knife, carefully slice the cakes in half horizontally.

Place a cake circle inside on the bottom of 1 of 10 glasses. Scatter a few strawberry halves, 4 blueberries, and 4 raspberries around the edge of the cake, arranging them so they are leaning against one another, flush against the glass. Spoon 1 tablespoon of strawberry sauce and 2 tablespoons of the lemon cream over them.

Place a cake circle over the cream, patting it down very gently to fit it into the glass. (It's fine if there are gaps between the layers.) Scatter a few strawberry halves, 4 blueberries, and 4 raspberries around the edge of the cake. Spoon 1 tablespoon of the boysenberry sauce over them, followed by 2 tablespoons of lemon cream, and a tablespoon of strawberry sauce over that. Arrange another layer of fruit around the edge of the cake. Place the final layer of cake over the fruit. Spoon a tablespoon of boysenberry sauce over the cake, allowing it to run down the inside of the glass. Spoon 1 tablespoon of lemon cream and 2 tablespoons of whipped cream over the cake. Continue in the same manner with the remaining ingredients and chill for about an hour, but not overnight.

When you're ready to serve the cakes, scatter a teaspoon of the sliced almonds over them and sift a fine layer of powdered sugar on top.

YIELD: 10 cakes

CHOCOLATE BRIOCHE
CLUB SANDWICH

"Chocolate Brioche Club Sandwich" is just a fancy name for a not-so-fancy chocolate bread pudding. First baked in a loaf pan, it's chilled overnight before being sliced into thin sandwiches and heated for a final time before serving.

If you bake your own brioche, use the same Pyrex loaf pan to assemble and bake the chocolate-brioche club sandwich. If you buy your brioche, you'll need to make the proper size adjustments. When buying your cocoa powder and chocolate, try to find Scharffen Berger, Valrhona, or Chocolates El Rey.

To make the bread easier to slice, you may want to freeze the loaf for an hour or so.

TO MAKE THE CUSTARD: In a medium saucepan, over medium heat, combine the milk, cream, cardamom seeds, and cinnamon sticks. Using a small paring knife, split the vanilla bean in half lengthwise, and with the back of the knife, scrape out the pulp and the seeds; add the scrapings and the pod to the mixture. Bring it to a boil, and remove from the heat. Allow it to steep for about 30 minutes, and discard the cinnamon stick and vanilla-bean pod. Bring back to a boil and immediately remove from the heat.

In a large bowl, whisk together the eggs and the yolk. Slowly add the cream mixture to the eggs, stirring constantly. Whisk the chocolate in until it's melted. Strain the mixture through a fine-mesh sieve. Add the sugar, to taste.

Adjust the oven rack to the middle position, and preheat the oven to 300 degrees.

TO MAKE THE SOAKING LIQUID: In a medium bowl, whisk to combine the milk, cream, cocoa powder, and sugar. Pour the liquid into a shallow rectangular dish.

Using a serrated knife, slice off all of the crust of the brioche loaf. Cut the bread crosswise into 3 ½-inch-thick slices, and set aside the scraps for another use.

1 Brioche Loaf (see page 217),
or a 1-pound loaf of
store-bought brioche

FOR THE CUSTARD
1 cup whole milk
1 cup heavy cream
4 pods cardamom, seeds removed
from their pods and crushed
2 cinnamon sticks
1 vanilla bean
2 extra-large eggs
1 extra-large egg yolk
4 ounces bittersweet chocolate,
finely chopped
1–2 tablespoons sugar

FOR THE SOAKING LIQUID
1 cup whole milk
1 cup heavy cream
½ cup unsweetened cocoa powder
3 tablespoons sugar

1 cup heavy cream, to pour around
the edges of the sandwich

Place one of the brioche slices in the soaking liquid, and press it gently with your fingertips to help it absorb the liquid. Carefully turn it over, and press it again with your fingertips. The brioche should be very spongy and thoroughly saturated.

Pour a layer of custard into a 6-cup-capacity (8½-by-4½-by-2½-inch) Pyrex or ceramic loaf pan, just enough to cover the bottom of the pan. Transfer the soaked slice of brioche to the pan, and pour a layer of custard over it, enough to cover it. (If the bread is too soft to pick up in one piece, cut it in half and then transfer it.) Soak another piece of bread in the same manner, and place in the loaf pan. Pour a layer of custard over it, and repeat the process with the third piece of bread, pouring the remaining custard over the top, so that it comes up to ¼ inch below the rim of the loaf pan.

Cover the pan tightly with a piece of aluminum foil domed in the center, so it doesn't come into contact with the custard. Prick the foil a few times with a fork, so steam can escape. Place the loaf pan in a baking dish, and fill the baking dish with 1 inch of water. Bake for 1 hour, until the custard is set. Remove from the water bath. Carefully remove the foil, and allow it to cool. Cover the pan with plastic wrap, and chill overnight or up to 5 days.

Before serving, preheat the oven to 400 degrees.

Fill the sink with about an inch of hot water. Put the loaf pan in the water and allow it to sit there for a minute or two to help loosen it from the pan. Run a knife around the edges of the pan, and invert the pudding onto a flat surface. Cut the sandwich into about 10 ¾-inch-thick slices.

Place each slice on an ovenproof plate, and heat in the oven for 5 minutes. Pour a few tablespoons of cream around the edge of the sandwich.

YIELD: 10 slices

OPEN-FACED BERRY BRIOCHE SANDWICH

French toast never had it so good. Slices of buttery brioche are drenched in a cassis (black-currant) custard, then coated with sugar and fried until crisp. Served with a spoonful each of tangy Greek yogurt and cassis compote, this breakfast favorite doubles as an elegant dessert.

If you don't have time to bake your own brioche, choose an egg bread or country-style white bread that is soft in texture. If you can't find black currants, make the berry compote instead, using boysenberries or blackberries.

TO MAKE THE CASSIS OR BERRY COMPOTE: Place the sugar in a medium saucepan. Add 2 tablespoons of the water for the cassis compote or 1 tablespoon if you're making the berry compote and stir until the sugar resembles wet sand. Using a small paring knife, split the vanilla bean lengthwise. With the back of the knife, scrape out the pulp and the seeds, and add the scrapings and the pod to the pan. Over medium heat, cook the mixture until it turns a light caramel, washing down the sides of the pan with a brush dipped in water to dissolve the sugar granules. Add half of the berries (and the juice if you're using frozen ones). The caramel will seize and harden. Continue cooking until the caramel is halfway melted, stirring with a wooden spoon. Turn off the heat, and continue stirring until the caramel is completely melted.

If you're using black currants, pour the mixture into the bowl of un-cooked currants, stirring gently so as not to break up the berries. Taste, and adjust the sweetness if necessary; the compote should be tart.

If you're using blackberries or boysenberries, strain the mixture over a bowl. Add the strained berries to the uncooked berries, and pour the juice back into the saucepan. Bring the juice to a boil and remove it from the heat. In a small bowl, combine the remaining water with the cornstarch. Whisk the cornstarch mixture into the berry juice. Return the pan to the heat, and

FOR THE CASSIS COMPOTE
1 cup sugar
2 tablespoons water
1 vanilla bean
2 cups (10 ounces) fresh black cur-rants or unsweetened frozen ones, thawed, with their juice

FOR THE BERRY COMPOTE
¾ cup sugar
3 tablespoons water
1 vanilla bean
About 10 cups (2½ pounds) fresh boysenberries or blackberries or unsweetened frozen ones, thawed, juice reserved
1 tablespoon plus 1½ teaspoons cornstarch

FOR THE SOAKING LIQUID
6 cups (about 1 pound 12 ounces) fresh or frozen black currants, blackberries, or boysenberries or unsweetened frozen ones, completely thawed, juice reserved
2 extra-large eggs, beaten well
1 cup plus 2 tablespoons heavy cream
½ cup sugar
¾ teaspoon pure vanilla extract

bring back to a boil, whisking constantly. Pour the hot liquid over the berries, stirring gently so as not to break them up. Taste, and adjust the sweetness if necessary (the compote should be tart).

TO MAKE THE SOAKING LIQUID: In the bowl of a food processor fitted with a metal blade, pulse the fruit (and juice if you're using frozen berries) until just puréed. Place the purée in a fine-mesh sieve set over a bowl, and press the fruit through, straining out the seeds and skin. (You should have about 1½ cups of juice after straining.) Whisk in the eggs, cream, sugar, and vanilla extract.

Preheat the oven to 400 degrees.

Cut the brioche loaf into 4 1-inch-thick slices, reserving the rest for another use.

Place one of the slices in the soaking liquid, and press it gently with your fingertips to help it absorb the liquid. Carefully turn it over and press it again with your fingertips. It should be very spongy and thoroughly saturated. Remove the bread from the bowl, scraping the slice against the edge of the bowl to remove the excess liquid. Place it on a piece of parchment paper or on a plate, and sprinkle one side with 2 tablespoons of sugar. Repeat with the other slices of bread.

In a small non-stick skillet, melt about 2 tablespoons of the clarified butter over medium-high heat. When the butter is very hot and bubbly, place 1 slice of the bread, sugared side down, in the skillet, and cook for about 2 minutes, until it's crisp but not burned. Sprinkle the top surface of the bread with 2 tablespoons of sugar, and carefully flip it over to cook on the other side for a minute or two. Transfer it to a baking sheet, and continue frying the remaining slices in the same manner, adding more clarified butter as necessary.

Bake them in the oven for about 10 minutes, until the slices of bread puff up slightly in the center. Cut each piece in half on the diagonal.

Spoon about ¼ cup of yogurt onto the center of each plate, smoothing it into a circle. Place 2 of the bread halves in the center, leaving some yogurt exposed. Spoon about 1 tablespoon of compote over the center of the bread, allowing it to drip over the edge, into the yogurt.

YIELD: 4 servings

1 Brioche Loaf (see page 217) or a 1-pound loaf of store-bought brioche
½ cup Clarified Butter (see page 201)
Scant ½ cup sugar, for sprinkling
1 cup Greek-style yogurt or full fat yogurt

ALMOST OREOS

When I first tried to copy an Oreo cookie, I made three major mistakes: they weren't dark enough, they didn't have the right flavor, and they didn't pass the milk test. It wasn't until somewhere around my 4,999th try that things took a turn for the better. As I pulled my cookies out of the oven, I knew right away that the color was finally right. After I filled them, I crossed my fingers and took a bite. My eyes filled with tears. The only thing these cookies lacked was a tall, cold glass of milk.

To get that deep, nearly black color, you'll need to use some highly alkalized black cocoa powder (see King Arthur Flour in the sources) for color, and some unsweetened Dutch-process cocoa powder for flavor. When buying your unsweetened cocoa powder and chocolate, look for Scharffen Berger or Valrhona.

There's so much chocolate in this dough, it's best to roll and cut the cookies out as soon as it's made; otherwise the dough will become brittle and too difficult to cut. (If you don't want to bake all of the cookies, refrigerate or freeze them after you cut them out, and bake them at a later date.) Watch them carefully as they bake. This dough is so dark, it's hard to tell the difference between a perfectly crisp cookie and an overdone, burned cookie. The stark white filling must be cooked and cooled to the correct temperature to get a smooth, chewy consistency.

In a food processor fitted with a metal blade, grind the cocoa nibs to a coarse consistency, slightly larger than grains of rice.

In the bowl of an electric mixer fitted with the paddle attachment, cream the butter, baking soda, salt, and cocoa nibs on low speed for 2–3 minutes, until softened. Turn the mixer off, and add the sugars and cocoa powders. Turn the mixer up to medium speed, and mix another minute or two, until the mixture is light and fluffy, scraping down the sides of the bowl as needed. Add the melted chocolate and vanilla extract, and mix for another minute. Turn the mixer off, and add the flour. Mix on low just to combine.

Adjust the oven racks to the lower and middle positions, and preheat the oven to 300 degrees.

Divide the dough in half.

FOR THE COOKIES
3 tablespoons cocoa nibs
(optional; see sources)
1½ sticks (6 ounces) unsalted butter
1 teaspoon baking soda
½ teaspoon kosher salt
½ cup plus 3 tablespoons light-brown sugar, lightly packed
½ cup plus 3 tablespoons granulated sugar
5 tablespoons black, super-alkalized cocoa powder (see sources) plus 3 tablespoons unsweetened cocoa powder
6 ounces bittersweet chocolate, melted and kept warm
1 tablespoon pure vanilla extract
1¾ cups unbleached all-purpose flour

FOR THE FILLING
2 cups granulated sugar
½ cup water
½ teaspoon fresh lemon juice
1 tablespoon corn syrup
Scant ½ teaspoon kosher salt
1 vanilla bean

FOR SERVING
1 pitcher ice-cold milk

Roll one half of the dough out between 2 sheets of parchment paper to ⅛-inch thickness. Transfer the dough to a baking sheet, and chill no longer than 5 minutes to remove the paper.

Roll out the other half of the dough in the same manner, and chill.

Remove the top pieces of the parchment paper. Using a 2½-inch round, fluted cookie cutter, cut out the circles as closely together as possible. Remove the cookies with a spatula, and place them ½ inch apart on 2 or 3 parchment-lined baking sheets. Gather the scraps, roll the dough out, and cut out the circles in the same manner.

Using a 1-inch fluted cookie cutter, create a decorative pattern by making six overlapping designs (not cutting all the way through the dough) around the perimeter of each cookie, about ¼ inch away from the edge. Using a skewer, mark a dot in the center of each "flower"-shaped design.

Bake the cookies for about 25–30 minutes, rotating the baking sheets halfway through baking.

TO MAKE THE FILLING: In a small heavy-duty saucepan, combine the sugar, water, lemon juice, corn syrup, and salt. Using a small paring knife, split the vanilla bean in half lengthwise. With the back of the knife, scrape out the pulp and the seeds, and add the scrapings and the pod to the mixture. Bring the syrup to a boil over medium-high heat, washing down the sides of the pan with a brush dipped in water, as necessary, to dissolve the sugar granules. Cook the syrup until it reaches the soft-ball stage, about 242 degrees on a candy thermometer.

Pour the syrup into the bowl of an electric mixer. (Any speck of grit or lint from a kitchen towel could cause the filling to crystallize, so clean the bowl thoroughly and allow it to air-dry as well as possible.) Allow the syrup to cool to 140 degrees, and remove and discard the vanilla pod.

Using the paddle attachment (making sure it's very clean as well), mix the filling on medium speed for 3–5 minutes, until it becomes white. (If it's overmixed, the filling will harden.) Keep in a warm place until you're ready to use it.

TO FILL THE COOKIES: Flip half of the cookies over, so the patterned side is face-down.

Place the filling in a plastic pastry bag with a small opening. Pipe a circle of filling around the perimeter of the bottom cookie, about ¼ inch from the edge, and pipe a dot of filling in the center. Sandwich the 2 cookies together, and continue with the remaining cookies. (If the filling stiffens and becomes difficult to work with, warm it in a microwave oven for no longer than 6 seconds.)

Alternatively, between the palms of your hands, roll 2 teaspoons of the filling into a ball, and, using your fingertips, press it into a disc slightly smaller than the cookie. Place the filling discs on the bottom cookies. Place the top cookies over them, pressing the 2 sides gently together.

Serve the cookies with a cold glass of milk.

YIELD: About 2 dozen cookies

CHOCOLATE CARAMEL FANCY SANDWICH COOKIES

These are undoubtedly the prettiest sandwich cookies I've ever seen. As much a tart as a cookie, this special-occasion dessert has a ring of caramel dotted with a chocolate center and sandwiched between two crisp chocolate cookies. If you've ever tried Claudia Fleming's chocolate-caramel tarts at Gramercy Tavern in New York, then you'll know where the idea came from.

Start the caramel and hot fudge a few hours ahead, so they are thick and at room temperature when you fill the cookies. (Any leftover chocolate or caramel can be refrigerated and reheated to serve on ice cream.) For an extra-fancy cookie, dab some 22-karat edible gold specks (available at specialty baking shops or paint stores) over the chocolate center. When buying your cocoa powder and chocolate, try to find Scharffen Berger, Valrhona, or Chocolates El Rey.

TO PREPARE THE CARAMEL: In a small saucepan, over low heat, combine the cream and butter. Using a small paring knife, split the vanilla bean lengthwise. With the back of the knife, scrape out the pulp and the seeds, and add the scrapings and the pod to the butter and cream. Cook the mixture until the butter melts.

In a small heavy-duty saucepan, over medium heat, cook the corn syrup until it's bubbly. Add a tablespoon or so of the sugar, stirring constantly. Don't allow the mixture to darken in color. When the sugar has melted completely and the mixture is bubbling around the edges, add another tablespoon or so of sugar. Continue in this manner until all of the sugar has been added. The mixture will become opaque, grainy, and slightly thickened. Cook it for 3–4 more minutes, stirring and swirling the pan, until the caramel is thick and has turned a light-golden straw color. The entire process will take up to 20 minutes.

Remove the caramel from the heat, and stir in the butter-and-cream

FOR THE CARAMEL

½ cup heavy cream

3 tablespoons unsalted butter

½ vanilla bean

2 tablespoons corn syrup

1 cup granulated sugar

1 tablespoon crème fraîche
or sour cream

FOR THE CHOCOLATE

2 tablespoons granulated sugar

2 tablespoons corn syrup

¼ cup water

¼ cup plus 2 tablespoons
unsweetened cocoa powder

1 teaspoon instant coffee

4 ounces bittersweet chocolate,
finely chopped

1 tablespoon dark rum

FOR THE COOKIES

2 sticks (½ pound) unsalted butter

1 teaspoon kosher salt

½ cup granulated sugar

¼ cup plus 1 tablespoon light-brown
sugar, lightly packed

½ cup imported unsweetened
cocoa powder, plus extra for sifting
over tops of cookies

mixture. It will bubble up and spatter, so be careful as you pour. Return the saucepan to medium heat, and cook the caramel for another 3–5 minutes, until it has turned a deep golden-brown color. Remove it from the heat, and stir in the crème fraîche. Transfer the caramel to a bowl to cool, and remove the vanilla bean and discard it.

TO PREPARE THE CHOCOLATE: In a small heavy-duty saucepan, whisk together the sugar, corn syrup, water, cocoa powder, and coffee over medium heat. Bring the mixture to a boil for 1–2 minutes, stirring constantly to prevent it from burning on the bottom. Remove the pan from the heat, and whisk in the chocolate. Bring the mixture back to a boil, and reduce it for a minute or so, whisking constantly, until the chocolate is completely melted. Remove the pan from the heat, and stir in the rum. The mixture should be shiny and smooth. Transfer it to a bowl to cool to room temperature.

TO MAKE THE COOKIES: In the bowl of an electric mixer fitted with the paddle attachment, cream the butter and salt on low speed for 2–3 minutes, until softened. Add the sugars, and mix on medium speed for another 3–4 minutes, until the mixture is light and fluffy, scraping down the sides of the bowl as needed. Turn the mixer off, and add the cocoa powder and cornstarch. Turn the mixer on low, and mix for a minute to incorporate.

Measure out 2 teaspoons from one of the egg yolks, and discard the rest of that yolk. Combine it with the other, whole yolk, and whisk in the vanilla extract. Add to the butter mixture, and mix on low speed for 1 minute to incorporate. Turn the mixer off, and add the flour. Turn the mixer to low speed, and mix for about 1 minute, until the flour is just combined.

Divide the dough in half, and flatten into 2 discs. Chill it for about 15 minutes, until firm.

Adjust the oven racks to the upper and lower positions, and preheat the oven to 350 degrees.

TO ROLL OUT THE BOTTOMS: Remove one half of the dough from the refrigerator. On a lightly floured surface, roll the dough out to ⅛-inch thickness, flouring the surface as necessary. Brush off the excess flour. Using a 2¼-inch round cookie cutter, cut out the circles as closely together as possible. Place them ½ inch apart on a parchment-lined baking sheet. Gather the

¼ cup cornstarch

2 extra-large egg yolks

1½ teaspoons pure vanilla extract

2 cups unbleached pastry flour or unbleached all-purpose flour

1–2 teaspoons fleur de sel

1 sheet edible gold leaf (optional)

scraps, roll out the dough, cut out more cookies, and place on the baking sheet in the same manner. Chill for about 10 minutes, until firm.

TO ROLL OUT THE TOPS: Remove the second half of the dough from the refrigerator. Roll it out, cut out the cookies, and place them on a baking sheet in the same manner as the bottoms. Using a 1¼-inch round cookie cutter, cut out the centers of the top cookies. (Reserve and bake the cut-out centers into tiny button cookies, or gather them together, chill, and reroll to use for additional large cookies.)

TO BAKE THE BOTTOMS: Bake for 18–20 minutes, rotating the baking sheet halfway through.

TO BAKE THE TOPS: Bake for about 15 minutes, rotating the sheet halfway through.

Allow the cookies to cool completely.

Flip the bottoms over. Using a spoon or a pastry bag fitted with a #2 tip, pipe a ring of the caramel ¼ inch from the edge, leaving a 1-inch circular center for the chocolate.

Using a spoon or a pastry bag fitted with a #2 tip, fill the centers of the cookies with the chocolate. (Each cookie gets about 1 teaspoon of chocolate and 1 teaspoon of caramel.)

Sift a fine layer of cocoa powder over the cookie tops. Center the tops over the bottoms, cocoa-powder side facing up. Sprinkle the chocolate center with a few grains of fleur de sel. Dab a very small fleck of gold leaf over the chocolate if you like.

YIELD: 25–30 cookies

Lemon Hats

Most decorative cookies are flat and one-dimensional, their shape defined by the cookie cutter. Though cut out with round cookie cutters, these lemon cookies are stacked into three-dimensional constructions. The larger, bottom cookie makes a brim, while the smaller cookie crown on top sandwiches the lemon curd in between. Accessorized with a fennel-frond feather, these Lemon Hats will never go out of fashion.

TO MAKE THE LEMON-CURD FILLING: In a medium stainless-steel or other non-reactive heatproof bowl, whisk together the lemon juice, lemon zest, lime juice, lime zest, egg, egg yolk, and sugar.

Bring a pot of water to a gentle simmer. Place the bowl over the pot, making sure that the bowl isn't touching the water. Rotate the bowl from time to time, and stir the mixture occasionally. Cook it for about 25 minutes, until it's very thick.

Using a fine-mesh sieve, strain the lemon curd, and cool to room temperature.

Transfer the mixture to a blender or a food processor fitted with a metal blade. Add the butter 2 tablespoons at a time, mixing a few seconds after each addition, just long enough to incorporate the butter. Chill the curd for 30 minutes to an hour, or up to 2 days.

TO MAKE THE COOKIE DOUGH: In a small skillet, over medium-high heat, toast the fennel seeds until they release their aroma. In a spice grinder or a mortar and pestle, grind the seeds coarsely.

In a food processor fitted with a metal blade, process the almonds and half of the powdered sugar until they're a fine meal. Add the cornmeal and fennel seeds, and pulse to combine.

In the bowl of an electric mixer fitted with the paddle attachment, cream the butter and lemon zest on low speed for about 2 minutes. Turn the mixer off, and add the almond mixture and remaining powdered sugar. Turn the mixer up to medium, and mix another 3–4 minutes, until the mixture is light and fluffy, scraping down the sides of the bowl as needed. Add the egg yolks one at a time, mixing the first in well before adding the second. Turn the

FOR THE LEMON CURD FILLING

2 tablespoons plus 2 teaspoons
lemon juice

2 teaspoons lemon zest

2 tablespoons plus 2 teaspoons
lime juice

2 teaspoons lime zest

1 extra-large egg

1 extra-large egg yolk

¼ cup granulated sugar

1½ ounces unsalted butter,
slightly softened

FOR THE COOKIES

1 teaspoon fennel seeds

1 cup (2½ ounces) whole
unblanched almonds

½ cup plus 1 tablespoon powdered
sugar, plus extra for sifting
over the cookies

3 tablespoons fine yellow cornmeal

1 stick (4 ounces) unsalted butter

1 tablespoon plus 2 teaspoons
finely chopped lemon zest

2 extra-large egg yolks

1 cup unbleached pastry flour or
unbleached all-purpose flour

16–32 small fennel-frond sprigs

mixer off, and add the flour in 3 batches, mixing on low speed until it's just combined.

Gather two-thirds of the dough into a ball, and flatten it into a disc to use for the bottom cookies. Gather the remaining dough into a ball, and flatten into a disc to use for the top cookies. Wrap the discs with plastic, and chill them for about 30 minutes to an hour, until firm.

Adjust the oven racks to the lower and middle positions, and preheat the oven to 350 degrees.

TO ROLL OUT THE BOTTOMS: Remove the larger piece of dough from the refrigerator. On a lightly floured surface, roll the dough out until it's $\frac{1}{8}$ inch thick. Using a $2\frac{1}{2}$-inch round cookie cutter, cut out the cookies as closely together as possible, and place them $\frac{1}{2}$ inch apart on 1–2 parchment-lined baking sheets. Gather the scraps, roll out the dough, and cut out more cookies in the same manner. Chill them for about 10 minutes, until firm.

TO ROLL OUT THE TOPS: On a lightly floured surface, roll out the remaining dough until it's $\frac{1}{4}$ inch thick. Using a $1\frac{1}{2}$-inch round cookie cutter, cut out the cookies, cutting as closely together as possible, and place them $\frac{1}{2}$ inch apart on a parchment-lined baking sheet. Gather the scraps, roll out the dough, and cut out more cookies in the same manner. Using a $\frac{3}{4}$-inch round cookie cutter, cut out the centers of the cookie tops. (Reserve and bake the cut-out centers into tiny button cookies, or gather them together, chill, and reroll to use for additional cookies.) Chill tops for about 10 minutes, until firm.

TO BAKE THE BOTTOMS: Bake for about 15 minutes, rotating the baking sheet halfway through.

TO BAKE THE TOPS: Poke the ends of the fennel fronds (you may need more than one frond) into each cookie top, and bake for about 18–20 minutes, rotating the baking sheet halfway through. Allow the cookies to cool for at least 30 minutes.

Flip the bottoms over. Using a spoon or a pastry bag fitted with a #2 tip, spoon or pipe about 1 teaspoon of the lemon filling onto the center of each bottom cookie.

Sift a fine layer of powdered sugar over the tops. Center the top cookie over the filling, and press it down gently.

YIELD: 22 cookies

NOT NUTTER BUTTERS

I knew my days as a Girl Scout had finally paid off when I was able to duplicate my favorite peanut-butter cookies. Whether peanut-shaped like a nutter butter or cut into circles as do-si-dos, their comforting flavor and soft crunch is like no other. And you'll never have to wait and wonder when Girl Scout cookie season is coming again.

TO MAKE THE COOKIES: In a medium skillet, melt 1 stick of the butter over medium heat. Using a small paring knife, split the vanilla bean lengthwise. With the back of the knife, scrape out the pulp and the seeds, and add the scrapings and the pod to the butter. Add the oats, and cook for 5–7 minutes, stirring constantly, until the oats are lightly toasted and a golden-brown color. Transfer to a bowl, discard the vanilla pod, and chill the oat mixture.

In the bowl of an electric mixer fitted with the paddle attachment, cream the remaining butter, the baking soda, and salt on low speed for 2–3 minutes, until the butter is softened. Add the sugars, and mix on medium speed until the mixture is light and fluffy, scraping down the sides of the bowl as needed. Add the peanut butter, and mix to combine. Turn the mixer off, and add the oat mixture and the flour. Turn the mixer to low speed, and mix for another minute, until the ingredients are incorporated and the dough pulls away from the sides of the bowl and comes together into a ball.

FOR THE PEANUT-SHAPED COOKIES: Using your hands, roll the dough into 1-inch balls. On the work surface, roll one of the balls back and forth, tapering the ends to form a 1½-inch-long football-shaped oval with slightly pointed ends. Continue in the same manner with the remaining dough.

Place 2 of the oval shapes on a parchment-lined baking sheet, with the points touching. Using the palm of your hand, applying even pressure, flatten them so that the adjacent ends of the 2 ovals join together and create a peanut shape, 3 inches long and just under ¼ inch thick. Repeat with the remaining dough, placing the cookies 2½ inches apart on the baking sheet.

FOR THE COOKIES
3 sticks (12 ounces) unsalted butter
1 vanilla bean
2 cups quick-cooking rolled oats
2 teaspoons baking soda
2 teaspoons kosher salt
¾ cup granulated sugar
¾ cup light-brown sugar
¾ cup natural, chunky-style unsalted peanut butter, excess oil poured off and discarded
2¼ cups unbleached all-purpose flour

FOR THE FILLING
6 tablespoons (3 ounces) unsalted butter
1½ teaspoons kosher salt
¼ cup plus 2 tablespoons powdered sugar
1 cup plus 2 tablespoons natural, chunky-style unsalted peanut butter

Using a straight-edge razor blade or a knife, mark diagonal crisscross patterns over the surface of each cookie. Chill them for about 15 minutes, until firm.

FOR THE ROUND COOKIES: Using your hands, roll the dough into 2-inch balls. Place the balls on a parchment-lined baking sheet, $2\frac{1}{2}$ inches apart. Using the heel of your hand, flatten the balls into $2\frac{1}{2}$–3-inch discs. Using a fork, mark diagonal crisscross patterns over the surface of each cookie. Chill them for about 15 minutes, until firm.

Adjust the oven racks to the lower and middle positions, and preheat the oven to 350 degrees.

Bake the cookies for about 18–20 minutes, until lightly browned and slightly firm to the touch, rotating the baking sheets halfway through. Allow them to cool.

TO MAKE THE FILLING: In the bowl of an electric mixer fitted with the paddle attachment, cream the butter and salt on medium speed for about 1 minute, until the butter is softened. Add the sugar and peanut butter, and mix for another minute to combine them.

TO FILL THE PEANUT-SHAPED COOKIES: Roll a teaspoon of filling into a ball and, using your fingertips, press it into a disc. Continue with the remaining filling.

Flip half of the cookies over to make the bottoms. Place a disc of filling on each end of the peanut shape. Place the top cookies over the filling, pressing the sides together gently to sandwich them together.

TO FILL THE ROUND COOKIES: Roll 2 teaspoons of the filling into a ball and, using your fingertips, press it into a disc. Continue with the remaining filling.

Flip half of the cookies over to make the bottoms. Place a disc of filling in the center of each. Place the top cookies over the filling, pressing gently to sandwich them together.

YIELD: 36 cookies

PAIN D'ÉPICES PIGS

Can you call two or three pigs that are attached by a string (not a filling) a sandwich cookie? Probably not, but I love these spiced-bread pigs so much that I decided to include them anyhow.

For the mom pig, I use a special pig-shaped cookie cutter that's 7½ inches from snout to tail, and for the baby pig, I use a 3¼-inch pig-shaped cutter. And if you can find it, use a 2-inch pig-shaped cutter for the runt.

Adjust the oven racks to the lower and middle positions, and preheat the oven to 350 degrees.

In a small skillet, over medium-high heat, toast the fennel seeds and anise seeds for 3–4 minutes, until they release their aromas. In a spice grinder or a mortar and pestle, coarsely grind the seeds.

In a medium-sized saucepan, combine the honey, cream, brown sugar, fennel seeds, anise seeds, pepper, cardamom, nutmeg, 12 whole cloves, ground cloves, allspice, cinnamon, ground ginger, orange zest, and lemon zest. Over medium heat, bring the mixture to a boil and cook for about 15 minutes, until it reaches the soft-ball stage, or 240 degrees on a candy thermometer. Strain it through a fine-mesh sieve into a large bowl, and allow to cool.

Add the grated ginger, whiskey, and egg yolks, stirring well to combine.

Sift together the salt, baking powder, baking soda, and flours. Add to the honey mixture, stirring well to combine.

Turn the dough out onto a lightly floured surface. Gather two-thirds of the dough into a ball, and flatten it into a disc to use for the large-pig cookies. Gather the remaining dough, and flatten it into a disc to use for the small-pig cookies. Roll the dough out until it's approximately ½ inch thick, flouring the surface as needed. Brush off any excess flour. Cut out the larger pigs as closely together as possible, and place them on 2 parchment-lined baking sheets, allowing space for the smaller pigs. Gather the scraps, and continue to roll out the dough and cut out the cookies in the same manner.

1 tablespoon fennel seeds

2 tablespoons anise seeds

1½ cups honey

1 cup heavy cream

1 cup light-brown sugar

1 teaspoon black pepper

12 cardamom pods, seeds removed from the pods and crushed

1 tablespoon plus 1 teaspoon freshly grated nutmeg

12 whole cloves, plus about 16 for decorating

⅛ teaspoon ground cloves

2½ teaspoons ground allspice

1 tablespoon ground cinnamon

1 tablespoon plus 1 teaspoon ground ginger

2 wide strips orange zest

2 wide strips lemon zest

2 tablespoons grated fresh ginger

2 tablespoons whiskey

4 extra-large egg yolks

2½ teaspoons kosher salt

1 tablespoon baking powder

2½ teaspoons baking soda

4 cups plus 5 tablespoons unbleached all-purpose flour

½ cup plus 2 tablespoons whole-wheat flour

5 cinnamon sticks, for decorating

Do the same with the second disc of dough for the small pigs, and place them next to the larger pigs. You should have 8 large pigs and 8 small pigs. Gather the scraps, reroll, and cut out the runts (optional). Chill until firm.

For the big pigs' eyes, poke a whole clove into the dough where the eye would be. For the smaller pigs' eyes, break a small piece off a clove and poke it into the dough. For the tails, break 4 of the cinnamon sticks in half lengthwise—the pieces should be roughly 2½ inches long—and place them on the larger pigs, with the curly side facing up. Break the remaining cinnamon stick into quarters, and break off fragments of the stick to use as tails for the small pigs. Tie a piece of twine loosely around the neck of the large pig (allowing room for the dough to expand while baking, and allowing about 8 inches of string between the three pigs), and tie it around the necks of the smaller pigs to attach the three together.

Bake the cookies for about 25 minutes, rotating the sheets halfway through the baking. Bake until lightly browned, puffy, and slightly firm to the touch.

YIELD: 8 large pigs, 8 small pigs, and 8 runts

BAR SNACKS

When I decided to do sandwiches on Thursday night at Campanile, I envisioned an informal evening with a few people sitting around the bar, leisurely sipping wine and eating a simple meal. I imagined it as something between working and entertaining, cooking and chatting with friends (and fans) as they strolled in for a bite to eat. Well, was I ever wrong! They never strolled, they came in droves. Never quite fast enough to keep up with the hungry appetites, I was forced early on to expand my menu to include a few ready-to-eat, quick-fix bar snacks.

I hope you won't be as rushed as I am when you do sandwich night at your house. But that doesn't mean you can't invite your friends over a little early, offer them an aperitif, and leisurely entertain them over a few of these delicious bar snacks.

TINA'S GARDEN PICKLES

No bar menu is complete without a tart and vinegary pickle mix. Tina Wilson, a former chef at Campanile, offered me her quick and easy recipe for refrigerator pickles. Ready in just 24 hours, these crisp, delicious vegetables don't require months in the basement to set up.

In a medium skillet, over medium-high heat, toast the mustard seeds, fennel seeds, peppercorns, chiles, and bay leaves for 2–3 minutes, until the spices begin to release their aromas.

Place the above ingredients along with the water, vinegar, thyme, salt, and garlic in a medium saucepan over high heat, and bring to a boil. Reduce the heat to low, and simmer for 15 minutes.

Remove the pan from the heat, and stir in the shallots, cauliflower, carrots, fennel, celery, and bell pepper. Allow the mixture to cool, and pour it into a jar or bowl. Refrigerate the pickles for at least 24 hours.

YIELD: About 2½ cups

1 tablespoon mustard seeds

1 teaspoon fennel seeds

1 teaspoon black peppercorns

4 whole dried red chiles

2 bay leaves

3 cups water

1 cup champagne vinegar

2 3-inch sprigs fresh thyme

3 tablespoons kosher salt

3 garlic cloves, peeled and thinly sliced

2 or 3 shallots, peeled and cut into quarters with the root end intact

4 cauliflower florets (about 4 ounces), sliced into ¼-inch-thick slices

2 medium carrots (about 4 ounces), peeled and sliced on the extreme bias into ¼-inch-thick slices, or 5 baby carrots, cut in half vertically, with an inch of the green stems still intact

1 small fennel bulb (about 4 ounces), outer stalks removed, sliced lengthwise into ⅛-inch-thick slices

1 celery stalk, peeled and sliced on the extreme bias into ¼-inch-thick slices

1 small red or yellow bell pepper, sliced into ¼-inch-thick slices

CHEESE FRITTERS

These rich and satisfying two-bite fritters are crispy on the outside and soft and creamy in the center. Served with a green salad, they're a meal in themselves.

In a small saucepan, over medium-high heat, bring the milk, salt, and butter to a boil. Remove the pan from the heat, and whisk in all the flour at once. Return the mixture to the heat, and cook about 3 minutes, stirring constantly, until it draws back from the sides of the pan.

Remove the pan from the heat, and slowly add the eggs, 1 tablespoon at a time, stirring with a wooden spoon to incorporate each spoonful thoroughly before adding the next one. Stir in the mustard, and allow the mixture to cool completely.

Stir in the cheeses.

Fill a deep heavy-duty saucepan halfway with oil and heat the oil to 350 degrees, measuring the temperature with a deep-fat-frying thermometer.

TO FORM THE FRITTERS: Using a soupspoon, pick up a tablespoon or so of the dough. Holding a second soupspoon in the other hand, place it upside down over the spoonful of dough, with the handles of the spoons facing in opposite directions. Press down as you slide the spoons away from each other, scraping the dough onto the top spoon. Turn it over and repeat this action a few times, shaping and moving the dough back and forth between the 2 spoons, until you have formed a 1½-inch-long football-shaped oval. Using one of the spoons, scrape the fritter off onto a piece of parchment paper or wax paper. Continue in the same manner with the remaining dough.

Fry the fritters 4–6 at a time, being careful not to overcrowd them in the pan. Cook them for about 3 minutes, until nicely browned. Drain them on paper towels.

YIELD: 32 fritters

¼ cup whole milk

½ teaspoon kosher salt

1 stick (4 ounces) unsalted butter

¾ cup plus 2 tablespoons unbleached all-purpose flour

3 extra-large eggs, beaten

½ teaspoon Dijon mustard

2 ounces Stilton or another blue cheese, crumbled

2¼ cups (7 ounces) finely grated Gruyère or Fontina Val d'Aosta, Beaufort, aged Gouda, or Emmenthaler or a combination of any 3

Vegetable oil, for deep-frying

ALMONDS AND OLIVES MIX

Olive oil plays a major role in this tasty Spanish bar mix. First, blanched almonds are simmered in oil until they're a pale-caramel color. Next, whole garlic cloves are cooked in the same oil until golden and sweet. And, finally, the oil is used one last time to marinate the olives, imparting a rich, nutty flavor to the mix.

I've listed the olives that I prefer, but you can choose your own favorites, as long as they're firm and vary in color and flavor. Kalamatas are briny and plump. Lucques are fresh-tasting, narrow, and pale green. Picholines are meaty, round green olives. Oil-cured Moroccans have a jet-black, wrinkled texture, and Manzanillas are a slightly bitter Spanish variety. The optional caper berries, the brined, full-grown buds of the caper bush, add an occasional bite of salt and vinegar.

When you simmer the almonds, be careful not to overcook them or they'll become bitter. As you're cooking them, taste one for doneness and check that the color is a deep golden brown throughout the entire nut, without being burned. Remember they will continue cooking a bit as they cool, so take them off a few seconds early. If you don't want to fry the almonds, you can make a non-Spanish version of this snack by substituting toasted unblanched almonds.

1½ cups extra-virgin olive oil

¾ cup (4 ounces) blanched almonds (for simmering in oil) or unblanched almonds (for toasting in the oven)

1 teaspoon kosher salt

12–20 medium-sized whole garlic cloves, peeled

1 small lemon

1 small orange

2 whole dried red chiles

2 4-inch branches fresh rosemary

2 3-inch sprigs fresh thyme

8 black peppercorns, very coarsely crushed

2 bay leaves

3 ounces (approximately ½ cup) Kalamata olives

3 ounces (approximately ½ cup) Moroccan oil-cured olives

2 ounces (approximately ⅓ cup) Lucques olives

2 ounces (approximately ⅓ cup) Picholine olives

2 ounces (approximately ⅓ cup) Manzanilla olives

2 ounces (approximately ½ cup) caper berries (optional)

In a small sauté pan, over medium-low heat, bring the olive oil and almonds to a simmer. Cook the almonds for 8–10 minutes, stirring constantly, until they turn a light-caramel color.

Remove the pan from the heat and strain the almonds, reserving the oil. Spread the almonds out on a flat surface to cool. Toss with salt. (If you're toasting the almonds, preheat the oven to 325 degrees, toss the almonds with 1 teaspoon of oil and a little salt, and spread them on a baking sheet. Toast in the oven for 12–15 minutes.)

Return the oil to the saucepan. Over medium heat, toast the garlic cloves in the oil for about 3–5 minutes, until lightly browned. Strain and reserve the oil. Allow the oil to cool slightly, about 15 minutes.

Using a vegetable peeler, slice off a 4-inch-long, 1-inch-wide piece of lemon peel, using only the colored part, not the bitter white pith under-neath. Repeat with the orange.

Add the garlic cloves, chiles, lemon peel, orange peel, rosemary, thyme, peppercorns, bay leaves, olives, and caper berries to the oil, stirring to combine.

Before serving, transfer the olive mixture and some of the olive oil to a bowl, and scatter the almonds over the top. Sprinkle additional salt over the almonds.

N O T E : If you're not going to eat all of the mix the same day, add only enough nuts for the size serving you need, or they will get soggy. Stored in the oil, the olives and caper berries will keep for up to 1 month in the refrigerator (bring them to room tempera-ture before serving). The fried or toasted nuts will keep a few days stored separately in an airtight container.

Y I E L D : $2\frac{1}{2}$ cups

CANDIED SPICY WALNUTS

That inane expression "Betcha can't eat just one" probably originated after somebody tried one of these Candied Spicy Walnuts. Every Thursday night, before we open, I set up my pantry ingredients—tapenade, pesto, candied spicy walnuts, and braised vegetables— in little bowls along the bar in front of me. All night long, I have to slap away the hands of hungry customers repeatedly as they reach into my bowl of candied walnuts.

Spicy, salty, and sweet, these addictive nuts are delicious on their own or crumbled over the Gorgonzola, Radicchio, and Honey sandwich (page 74) or the Roasted Beets, Goat Cheese, and Sautéed Beet Greens sandwich (page 37). When frying the nuts, don't mistake their natural dark-mahogany color for a sign that they are burned. You will need to bite into one as they cook to make sure they're nicely browned throughout.

2 cups water

2 cups sugar

1¾ teaspoons cayenne pepper

2 cups (8 ounces) walnut halves

Vegetable oil, for deep-frying

1 teaspoon kosher salt

TO CANDY THE WALNUTS: In a large saucepan, over high heat, bring the water, sugar, and cayenne pepper to a boil. Using a pastry brush dipped in water, wash down the sides of the pan to remove any undissolved sugar granules.

Add the walnuts, turn the heat to medium-high, and simmer for about 20 minutes, reducing the syrup until it's thickened and the bubbles are large and bursting. The nuts will be very sticky. Drain half the nuts, leaving the other half of the nuts in the syrup over very low heat.

While the nuts are candying, fill a heavy-duty saucepan halfway with oil. Over medium heat, bring the oil up to 350 degrees, measuring the temperature on a deep-fat-frying thermometer. Carefully add the drained nuts, and fry them for about 2–3 minutes, stirring constantly, until they're well browned but not burned. Using a slotted spoon, transfer to a baking sheet to cool and sprinkle generously with salt. Drain and continue frying the remaining nuts.

You can store the nuts for a few days in an airtight container, or until they are no longer crisp.

YIELD: 2 cups

SPICED CARAMEL CORN

Cracker Jacks always come with a surprise. The surprise in my candied popcorn is the macadamia nuts and spices. This snack is for those diners who linger late on Thursday nights at Campanile and need a little something sweet to keep them going before I kick them out the door.

TO TOAST THE NUTS: Preheat the oven to 325 degrees. Spread the macadamia nuts on a baking sheet, and toast them in the oven for about 10–15 minutes, until they're lightly browned. Allow the nuts to cool, and coarsely chop them in half.

TO POP THE CORN: In a medium-sized pot, heat the oil over high heat. Add the popcorn, and cover with a lid. Once the corn begins to pop, shake the pan constantly. When the corn has finished popping, remove from the heat and take off the lid.

In a large deep pot, at least 12 inches wide, stir together the water, sugar, and corn syrup. Using a small paring knife, split the vanilla bean in half lengthwise. With the back of the knife, scrape out the pulp and the seeds, and add the scrapings and the pod to the mixture. Stir in the cinnamon, nutmeg, cloves, cardamom, and salt. Over medium-high heat, bring the mixture to a boil without stirring it. Using a pastry brush dipped in water, brush down the sides of the pan to remove any undissolved sugar granules.

Continue cooking over medium heat about 4–5 minutes, tilting and swirling the pan, until the mixture just begins to smoke and is a deep-caramel color. Stir in the popcorn and nuts, and continue to stir until the popcorn is completely coated, moving the skillet on and off the heat to prevent the caramel from burning. Cook the mixture until it turns a deep-mahogany color. Pour it onto a non-stick mat or parchment-lined baking sheet, and spread it out to cool. Remove and discard the vanilla bean.

It can be stored for up to 3 days in an airtight container.

YIELD: 8 servings

1 cup (4 ounces) whole macadamia nuts (optional)

½ teaspoon vegetable oil

⅓ cup unpopped popcorn

¼ cup water

2 cups sugar

2 tablespoons light corn syrup

1 vanilla bean

¾ teaspoon ground cinnamon

1½ teaspoons freshly grated nutmeg

⅛ teaspoon ground cloves

¼ teaspoon ground cardamom

1½ teaspoons kosher salt

HERB SALAD

Whenever people ask me what they should serve with a grilled-cheese sandwich, this is the salad I always recommend. Whether it's served as an accompaniment to a sandwich, a palate cleanser in between courses, or a digestive at the end of the meal, this salad's clean, crisp flavors are uplifting and refreshing. Assembled and piled on an oversized platter, it also makes a very pretty presentation at the table.

TO MAKE THE DRESSING: In a small bowl, combine the lemon juice and shallot, and allow them to sit for about 10 minutes. Whisk in the olive oil, salt, and pepper. Adjust the lemon juice, salt, and cracked black pepper to taste.

Separate out $\frac{1}{4}$ cup each of the dill, chervil, tarragon, and parsley leaves, and set aside. Finely chop the remaining quantity of herbs, and toss them together with all of the chives and the celery leaves.

TO ASSEMBLE THE SALAD: Place about a quarter of the lettuce leaves, slightly overlapping, on a large platter, and drizzle a few tablespoons of the dressing over them. Evenly scatter a quarter of the chopped herbs, a quarter of the whole herb leaves, and a sprinkling of fleur de sel over the lettuce.

Pile a second layer of lettuce leaves over the first, and continue layering in the same manner until you have used all of the lettuce, dressing, and herbs, finishing with a sprinkling of herbs and fleur de sel. Squeeze a little more lemon juice over the top, and several grindings of pepper, to taste.

YIELD: Serves 4

$\frac{1}{4}$ cup plus 2 tablespoons fresh
lemon juice
(about 3 lemons)
1 shallot, peeled and finely chopped
(about 1 tablespoon)
$\frac{1}{4}$ cup plus 2 tablespoons
extra-virgin olive oil
1 teaspoon kosher salt
Freshly cracked black pepper, to taste
$\frac{3}{4}$ cup fresh dill leaves,
stems removed
$\frac{3}{4}$ cup fresh chervil leaves,
stems removed
$\frac{3}{4}$ cup fresh tarragon leaves,
stems removed
$\frac{3}{4}$ cup fresh Italian parsley leaves,
stems removed
$\frac{1}{2}$ cup finely chopped fresh chives
2 or 3 heads Bibb lettuce, washed and
dried, with the bruised outer leaves
removed and discarded, and the
rest of the leaves separated
and kept intact
$\frac{1}{4}$ cup pale green celery
leaves (optional)
Fleur de sel or kosher salt, to taste

Melted Umbrian Pecorino

The subtle brilliance of this bar snack relies on the balance of the melted pecorino, sweet honey, and spicy chile. Since it's impossible to gauge how sweet your honey is and how spicy your chile seeds are, you'll have to make a trial version and decide on the exact proportions yourself.

Use shallow individual earthenware or ceramic baking dishes to melt the cheese in the oven—about 4 or 5 inches in diameter, or no more than ½ inch wider than the slices of cheese, to ensure that the cheese doesn't spread too thin when it melts. (If you don't have a small enough dish, bake two slices of cheese at a time in a larger dish.)

When I bite into this and close my eyes, it takes me back to one of my favorite Umbrian steak restaurants, Bistecaro in Panicarola.

1 baguette, cut on the bias
into ¼-inch-thick slices
1 or 2 whole dried red chiles
8 ounces fresh Pecorino di Pienza or
fresh Pecorino Toscano or Cacio di
Roma, sliced into 4 2-ounce slices,
about 4–5 inches wide and
¼ inch thick
Approximately 2 tablespoons chestnut, buckwheat, or corbezzola honey
Fleur de sel or kosher salt, to taste

Adjust the oven rack to the middle position, and preheat the oven to 450 degrees.

Grill the bread according to the directions on page 8.

Break the end off the chile, and pour out the seeds. (Reserve the rest of the chile for another use.)

Place a slice of cheese in each of the baking dishes (see headnote). Drizzle a teaspoon or so of honey over each slice of cheese, and sprinkle 8–10 chile seeds and a pinch of fleur de sel over each. Bake for 3–4 minutes, removing the dishes from the oven the moment the cheese begins to bubble, before it begins to brown, and spoon it onto some grilled bread, or eat it right out of the dish while it's creamy and piping hot.

YIELD: 4–8 servings

SPREADS AND CONDIMENTS

Condiments play a very important role in the sandwich world. They are the "supporting actors" in the cast of fillings that make the star ingredients taste even better. Whether it's a homemade rémoulade slathered on the bun of an Oyster Sandwich, a dollop of Salsa Romesco smeared beneath an olive-oil-fried egg, or an uneven layer of Green Goddess underneath the bacon, avocado, and watercress, the condiment is the essential element that completes the sandwich story.

Besides moistening the bread, my condiments add depth and color to the sandwiches they embellish. Concentrated in flavor, a tablespoon or two per sandwich is all you need of these rich, flavorful sauces. Sometimes I use them in the classic way by smearing the condiment over the bread, such as the aïoli that gets spread beneath the rare-seared tuna. Other times, I simply drizzle the condiment over the topping, such as the Parsley Basil Pesto that is spooned over the baked ricotta wedges. These condiments are so delicious, you can eat them on their own. Grill a slice of bread and spread some anchoïade over it; you'll never think of condiments as second-rate ingredients again.

The condiments that follow can be made a day or two ahead and stored in the refrigerator. Have them ready, so that when you're assembling the sandwiches, it's one less thing to worry about. If you don't use the entire batch, save it to use as a sauce or dip with another dish or sandwich. The Green Goddess and Rouille can also be used as party dips with blanched vegetables or crudités. These condiments should never go to waste. If you don't have time to make your own, most of them are available off the shelf or in the refrigerated deli section of specialty stores and well-stocked supermarkets.

Though most chefs probably wouldn't devote an entire chapter to condiments, these are so delicious that I knew they warranted their own special place in my book. Without these tasty, rich sauces, a sandwich could be a very dull meal indeed.

CLARIFIED BUTTER

Clarified butter is ideal for putting on the bread when grilling sandwiches in a skillet. When butter is slowly melted and cooked for several minutes over a low heat, the water content evaporates and the milk solids begin to separate. After the butter is cooked, the milk solids are removed and the butter itself is like a pure oil, capable of much higher cooking temperatures without burning. You'll still have that fresh, buttery flavor on the bread, without the burned-butter taste or the oily flavors that some cooking oils leave behind. Store the clarified butter in a covered container in the refrigerator for up to three weeks, so it's ready when your grilled-cheese craving hits.

2 sticks unsalted butter

In a small saucepan, over medium-low heat, warm the butter until it boils with large, loud, rapidly bursting bubbles. Continue cooking about 5 to 7 more minutes, until the butter becomes foamy and the bubbles are fewer and quieter. Remove from the heat to prevent browning, and transfer to a bowl to cool. Skim the foam off the top and pour out the clarified butter, leaving the milk solids at the bottom of the bowl.

Little did I know that my son Oliver's favorite closed-faced sandwich would become one of my favorite open-faced sandwiches, albeit with a few minor adjustments. Store-bought mayonnaise slathered between two slices of bread makes him swoon. I'm not a fan of sugary jarred mayonnaise, but a smearing of homemade aïoli or rémoulade on a slice of grilled bread is perfection to me. As Oliver learned at a young age, sometimes less is more. Spoon an uneven layer of mayonnaise over the bread, always leaving the edges of the bread exposed. Usually considered spreads to embellish a sandwich or dish, here these flavorful condiments have the starring role.

Making a small amount of mayonnaise or aïoli can be challenging, even for the most skilled chef. The process takes a little patience, but it's worth it in the end. If you follow these important tips, you'll save yourself time and frustration.

You can either make your mayonnaises and aïolis from start to finish, using a mortar and pestle, or cheat a little by finishing them off in an electric mixer. Using a mortar and pestle, first grind the garlic, salt, and yolk together until a smooth purée. (If you don't have a mortar and pestle, smash the garlic with the back of the knife, whisk together with the salt and egg yolk in a stainless-steel bowl, and proceed from there.) For the more impatient cook, start the mayonnaise out by hand in the mortar, and once you've incorporated about half of the oil and the mixture has developed a nice thick consistency, you can finish adding the oil (very slowly) to the mayonnaise in an electric mixer fitted with the whisk attachment. At the restaurant, we make our mayonnaises and aïolis using only a mortar and pestle and whisking in the oil patiently, drop by drop, by hand.

Whichever technique or utensil you choose, you'll need to keep in mind a few things. If the surface area of the bowl is too large, the mixture won't emulsify properly, so choose a medium-sized mortar or bowl. When you begin to add the oil, you must add it drop by drop, using a metal whisk, whisking the mixture vigorously the entire time, and waiting until the oil is completely incorporated before adding the next drop. When the mixture becomes too thick to whisk, add some of the liquid (vinegar, lemon juice, and water) called for in the recipe. Once all of the oil has been whisked in, taste the mayonnaise to see if it needs more lemon, vinegar, or salt, or needs to be thinned down with a splash of water.

Theoretically, one egg yolk should be enough to thicken and emulsify 1 cup of oil into a smooth and creamy mayonnaise. But if your mayonnaise starts to separate, or "break," you'll need to fix it. To do this, transfer the "broken" mayonnaise to another container, clean and dry your bowl, get another egg yolk, and slowly begin to add the "broken" batch, drop by drop, to the egg yolk. Once you've added all of that mixture and the sauce is smooth and creamy, begin to add the remaining oil, little by little, according to the recipe.

It's almost impossible to make less than a cup of mayonnaise. You'll have some left over after using it for sandwiches, but save the extra for up to a few days in the refrigerator to make a few Odds & Ends Focaccete (page 109).

Aïoli

Traditionally, an aïoli should be made with lots of garlic and extra-virgin olive oil. If you find the flavor too strong, you can use half olive oil and half vegetable oil (and a little less garlic, if you must).

2–3 garlic cloves, peeled and chopped (about 1 tablespoon)

1 teaspoon kosher salt

1 extra-large egg yolk

1 cup extra-virgin olive oil, or ½ cup extra-virgin olive oil and ½ cup vegetable oil

2 teaspoons champagne vinegar or white-wine vinegar

1–2 tablespoons fresh lemon juice

2–3 teaspoons warm water

Using a mortar and pestle, pulverize the garlic and salt to a smooth paste. (If you don't have a mortar and pestle, smash the garlic with the flat side of a chef's knife or a garlic press.)

If your mortar is too small to whisk the entire amount of oil in (or you don't have one), transfer the mashed garlic and salt to the bowl of an electric mixer or a medium stainless-steel bowl, and whisk in the egg yolk by hand. Slowly drizzle in the olive oil, drop by drop, whisking constantly. As the mixture begins to thicken, add a teaspoon of vinegar, a teaspoon of lemon juice, and a teaspoon of warm water.

Once you've added almost half of the oil, place the bowl in the mixer fitted with a whisk attachment and mix on medium speed. Or continue to whisk in the oil by hand. Pour the oil in a slow, steady trickle, scraping down the sides of the bowl as necessary. As the mixture thickens, add a little more of the lemon juice, vinegar, and water, and continue whisking until the remaining olive oil is completely incorporated and the sauce is thickened. Season with lemon juice and salt, to taste.

VARIATION

For Lemon Aïoli, replace the vinegar with extra lemon juice and a teaspoon or so of finely chopped lemon zest.

ANCHOÏADE

At Campanile, we use whole salt-packed anchovies from Italy. These tend to be purer in flavor than the fish packed in oil. Though a little harder to find, these meaty, plump fish are firm and fleshy. Look for them sold in bulk at Italian delis and well-stocked supermarkets. If you can't find them, you can substitute oil- or brine-packed anchovies. Be sure to rinse the salted anchovies under cool water before cleaning them.

1 garlic clove, peeled and chopped
(about 1½ teaspoons)

½ teaspoon kosher salt

4 3-inch salt-packed anchovies,
rinsed well, backbone removed,
coarsely chopped
(about 1½ tablespoons)

1 extra-large egg yolk

1 cup extra-virgin olive oil, or ½ cup
extra-virgin olive oil and ½ cup
vegetable oil

1 tablespoon champagne vinegar
or white-wine vinegar

1–2 tablespoons fresh lemon juice

2–3 teaspoons warm water

16 Niçoise olives, or 8–10 Moroccan
oil-cured olives, or 8–10 Nyons olives,
pits removed, sliced into
3 or 4 slivers (optional)

Using a mortar and pestle, pulverize the garlic, salt, and anchovies to a smooth paste. (If you don't have a mortar and pestle, smash the garlic and anchovies with the flat side of a chef's knife.)

If your mortar is too small to whisk the oil in (or you don't have one), transfer the mixture to the bowl of an electric mixer or a medium stainless-steel bowl. Whisk together the mashed garlic, salt, and anchovies and the egg yolk by hand. Slowly drizzle in the olive oil, drop by drop, whisking constantly. As the mixture begins to thicken, add a teaspoon of vinegar, a teaspoon of lemon juice, and a teaspoon of warm water.

Once you've added almost half of the oil, place the bowl in the mixer fitted with a whisk attachment and mix on medium speed. Or continue to whisk in the oil slowly by hand. Pour the oil in a slow, steady trickle, scraping down the sides of the bowl as necessary. As the mixture thickens, add a little more of the vinegar, lemon juice, and water, and continue whisking until the remaining olive oil is completely incorporated and the sauce is thickened.

Season with lemon juice and salt, to taste, and stir in the olives if you like.

Caper Onion Mayonnaise

Adjust the oven rack to the middle position, and preheat the oven to 350 degrees.

Place the onion on a baking sheet, tossing it with the vinegar to coat. Bake for about 20 minutes, until the onion is softened. Allow it to cool, and finely chop.

In the bowl of an electric mixer or in a medium stainless-steel bowl, whisk the egg yolk and salt by hand. Slowly drizzle in the oil, drop by drop, whisking constantly. As the mixture begins to thicken, add a teaspoon each of the lemon juice and water.

Once you've added almost half of the oil, place the bowl in the mixer fitted with a whisk attachment and mix on medium speed. Or continue to whisk in the oil by hand. Pour the oil in a slow, steady trickle, scraping down the sides of the bowl as necessary. As the mixture thickens, add a little more of the lemon juice and water, and continue whisking until the remaining oil is completely incorporated and the sauce is thickened.

Stir in the onions, parsley, and capers. Season with lemon juice and salt, to taste.

½ small red onion, peeled and
chopped into 1-inch squares
1 tablespoon balsamic vinegar
1 extra-large egg yolk
¼ teaspoon kosher salt
1 cup vegetable oil
2–3 teaspoons fresh lemon juice
2–3 teaspoons warm water
1 tablespoon finely chopped
fresh Italian parsley leaves
1 tablespoon capers, preferably salt-
packed, rinsed well and
finely chopped

Rémoulade

In the bowl of an electric mixer or in a medium stainless-steel bowl, whisk the egg yolk, salt, and mustard by hand. Slowly drizzle in the oil, drop by drop, whisking constantly. As the mixture begins to thicken, add a teaspoon each of the lemon juice and the water.

Once you've added almost half of the oil, place the bowl in the mixer fitted with a whisk attachment and mix on medium speed. Or continue to whisk in the oil by hand. Pour the oil in a slow, steady trickle, scraping down the sides of the bowl as necessary. As the mixture thickens, add a little more of the lemon juice and water, and continue whisking until the remaining oil is completely incorporated and the sauce is thickened.

Stir in the red onion, capers, cornichons, tarragon, and parsley. Season with lemon juice and salt, to taste.

1 extra-large egg yolk

¼ teaspoon kosher salt

½ teaspoon Dijon mustard

1 cup vegetable oil

1–2 teaspoons fresh lemon juice

2–3 teaspoons warm water

1 tablespoon red onion, peeled and finely chopped

2 teaspoons capers, preferably salt-packed, rinsed well and finely chopped

2 teaspoons finely chopped cornichons or gherkins

1 teaspoon finely chopped fresh tarragon leaves

2 teaspoons finely chopped fresh Italian parsley leaves

Green Goddess Dressing

In a small saucepan, over high heat, bring about 1 cup of water and a table-spoon of the salt to a boil. Cook the herbs for 1 minute in the boiling water. Drain and place in a small bowl of iced water to cool. Strain the herbs and wrap them in cheesecloth. Over a small bowl, squeeze them to extract the juice, reserving the liquid. Coarsely chop the herbs. Using a mortar and pestle, pulverize them into a smooth paste, then transfer to a small bowl. Or, alternatively, in a food processor fitted with a metal blade or in a blender, process the herbs until a smooth purée. (You won't get as smooth a texture as you would using a mortar and pestle.)

In the same mortar and pestle, pulverize the garlic, anchovy, and remaining salt into a smooth paste. (If you don't have a mortar and pestle, smash the garlic and anchovy with the flat side of a chef's knife.)

If your mortar is too small to whisk the oil in (or you don't have one), transfer the mixture to the bowl of an electric mixer or a medium stainless-steel bowl. Whisk together the mashed garlic, salt, and anchovy with the egg yolk by hand. Slowly drizzle in the oils, drop by drop, whisking constantly. As the mixture begins to thicken, add a teaspoon of lemon juice, a teaspoon of vinegar, and a teaspoon of the herb liquid.

Once you've added almost half of the oil, place the bowl in the mixer fitted with a whisk attachment and mix on medium speed. Or continue to whisk in the oil by hand. Pour the oil in a slow, steady trickle, scraping down the sides of the bowl as necessary. As the mixture thickens, add a little more of the lemon juice, vinegar, and herb liquid, and continue whisking until the remaining oil is completely incorporated and the sauce is thickened. Stir in the herbs, and season with lemon juice and salt, to taste.

1 tablespoon plus 1½ teaspoons kosher salt

Heaping ½ cup fresh tarragon leaves, loosely packed

½ cup finely chopped fresh chives, loosely packed

½ cup fresh chervil leaves, loosely packed

½ cup fresh Italian parsley leaves, loosely packed

½ cup fresh basil leaves (large leaves torn in half), loosely packed

1 garlic clove, peeled and finely chopped (about 1 teaspoon)

1 3-inch-long salt-packed anchovy fillet, rinsed well, backbone removed, finely chopped (about 1½ teaspoons)

1 extra-large egg yolk

¾ cup vegetable oil

¼ cup extra-virgin olive oil

2–3 teaspoons fresh lemon juice

2 teaspoons champagne vinegar or white-wine vinegar

ROUILLE

On a hot grill or directly on the stovetop over high heat, char the pepper over an open flame, turning frequently, until the skin is blackened on all sides and the flesh becomes tender. Place the pepper in a plastic bag or in a bowl covered tightly with plastic wrap to steam until cool enough to handle. Using a towel, wipe off the charred skin. Remove and discard the seeds and ribs, and reserve the liquid. Finely chop the pepper, and set aside.

Soak the bread in the vinegar until soft. Place the saffron in a small bowl, and pour about 2 teaspoons of boiling water over it.

Using a mortar and pestle, pulverize the garlic and salt to a smooth paste. (If you don't have a mortar and pestle, smash the garlic with the flat side of a chef's knife or in a garlic press.)

If your mortar is too small to whisk the oil in (or if you don't have one), transfer the mixture to the bowl of an electric mixer or a medium stainless-steel bowl. Whisk together the garlic and salt, the bread, and the egg yolk by hand. Slowly drizzle in the oil, drop by drop, whisking constantly. As the mixture begins to thicken, add the saffron and water, the lemon juice, and a little of the pepper liquid.

Once you've added almost half of the oil, place the bowl in the mixer fitted with a whisk attachment and mix on medium speed. Or continue to whisk in the oil by hand. Pour the oil in a slow, steady trickle, scraping down the sides of the bowl as necessary. As the mixture thickens, add a little more of the pepper liquid, and continue whisking until the remaining oil is completely incorporated and the sauce is thickened. Stir in the peppers, and season with lemon juice and salt, to taste.

1 medium (about 8 ounces) red bell pepper

1 slice white sourdough bread, crusts removed, torn into 1-inch pieces

2 teaspoons champagne vinegar or white-wine vinegar

Approximately 20 strands saffron

3 garlic cloves, peeled and finely chopped (about 1 tablespoon)

1 teaspoon kosher salt

1 extra-large egg yolk

1 cup extra-virgin olive oil

1–2 teaspoons fresh lemon juice

Salsa Romesco

Adjust the oven racks to the middle and upper positions, and preheat the oven to 350 degrees.

Drizzle the tomato halves with a teaspoon of the olive oil and a pinch of salt. Place the tomatoes, cut side down, on a baking sheet, and roast on the upper rack for 45 minutes to an hour, until they are soft and the skin has wrinkled and blackened slightly. Allow to cool, remove, and discard the skin.

In a very small ovenproof skillet, saucepan, or dish, combine approximately ¼ cup of the olive oil with the garlic cloves, to cover the cloves halfway. Roast in the oven on the middle rack about 20 minutes, until the garlic is soft and malleable. Allow to cool, and squeeze the pulp from the cloves. Reserve the oil and set aside.

Turn the oven down to 325 degrees.

Spread the almonds and hazelnuts on a baking sheet (in separate piles). Toast on the middle rack in the oven for 12–15 minutes, until lightly browned. Place the hazelnuts in a kitchen towel, and rub them together to remove the skins.

Meanwhile, on a hot grill or directly on the stovetop over high heat, char the pepper over an open flame, turning frequently, until the skin is blackened on all sides and the flesh becomes tender. Place the pepper in a plastic bag or in a bowl covered tightly with plastic wrap to steam until cool enough to handle. Using a towel, wipe off the charred skin. Remove and discard the seeds and ribs. Coarsely chop the pepper.

In a small skillet, over medium heat, warm the reserved olive oil from the garlic. When the oil is hot, fry the bread on both sides until lightly browned. Remove the bread to a paper towel to drain.

In a mortar and pestle, or in a food processor fitted with a metal blade, grind the nuts and bread until they form a coarse paste. Add the tomato, roasted pepper, vinegar, garlic pulp, cayenne pepper, and salt, and pulverize or process until smooth. Slowly pour in the remaining ¼ cup of olive oil, and stir or process until combined. Season with salt, to taste. It will keep in the refrigerator for up to 5 days.

1 small tomato, cut in half
Approximately ½ cup extra-virgin olive oil
1 teaspoon kosher salt
3 garlic cloves, unpeeled
1 heaping tablespoon unblanched almonds
1 heaping tablespoon hazelnuts
1 medium (8-ounce) red bell pepper
¼ slice white sourdough bread, toasted
1 tablespoon red-wine vinegar
⅛ teaspoon cayenne pepper

TAPENADE

Using a mortar and pestle, pulverize the anchovy, lemon zest, orange zest, garlic, and capers to a smooth paste. (If you don't have one, finely chop the ingredients and smash with a knife to purée.) Add 1 cup of the olives, and continue to pulverize into a paste. Coarsely chop the remaining olives, and add to the mixture.

Stir in the olive oil, lemon juice, and basil. Season with more lemon juice and pepper, to taste. The tapenade will keep for up to 2 weeks in the refrigerator.

1 3-inch-long salt-packed anchovy, rinsed well, backbone removed, finely chopped (about 1½ teaspoons)

1 teaspoon finely chopped lemon zest

½ teaspoon finely chopped orange zest

1 garlic clove, peeled

1 teaspoon capers, preferably salt-packed, rinsed well and finely chopped

1¼ cups black olives (about 9 ounces), preferably Nyons or Niçoise, pitted

¼ cup extra-virgin olive oil

1–2 teaspoons fresh lemon juice

4 large fresh basil leaves, finely chopped (about 1 tablespoon)

Freshly cracked black pepper, to taste

PESTOS

"Pesto" is derived from the Italian verb *pestare,* which means "to pound." A pestle, the tool used in conjunction with a mortar to pulverize herbs and garlic, shares the Latin origins of its name with that of the product that it makes: a pesto. If you don't already own a mortar and pestle, I urge you to go out and buy one right now. They're not expensive, and you will certainly get your money's worth, I promise. Choose a mortar and pestle large enough to accommodate all of the ingredients. When pestos are made in a food processor or blender, they become frothy and pale in color, and the action of the blade will heat up the raw garlic and cause it to become bitter. If you want my advice, sell your food processor at a garage sale and invest in a mortar and pestle.

Though basil is the traditional herb used for making pesto, I like to make different-flavored pestos using mint and parsley. To keep the herbs a bright-green color, don't add the lemon juice until just before serving. For an even richer pesto, substitute walnuts for pine nuts, or use half of each. If you're serving grilled bread with pesto, shave some Parmigiano-Reggiano or an aged sheep's-milk cheese over the top to add more flavor and dimension to this simple open-faced sandwich. Pesto will keep for about 2 weeks in the refrigerator.

Basil Pesto

Preheat the oven to 325 degrees.

Spread the pine nuts on a baking sheet, and toast in the oven for about 8–10 minutes, until lightly browned.

Using a mortar and pestle, pulverize the pine nuts, garlic, basil, and salt into a smooth paste. (If you don't have one, finely chop the ingredients and smash with a knife to purée.) Slowly drizzle in the olive oil, and add the Parmesan, mixing well to incorporate. Season with lemon juice and salt to taste, just before serving.

3 tablespoons pine nuts
2–3 garlic cloves, peeled and finely chopped (about 1 tablespoon)
¾ cup chopped fresh basil leaves
1 teaspoon kosher salt
½ cup extra-virgin olive oil
¼ cup (1 ounce) finely grated Parmigiano-Reggiano
2–3 teaspoons fresh lemon juice

Mint Pesto

Preheat the oven to 325 degrees.

Spread the pine nuts on a baking sheet, and toast in the oven for about 8–10 minutes, until lightly browned.

Using a mortar and pestle, pulverize the pine nuts, garlic, mint, parsley, and salt to a smooth paste. (If you don't have one, finely chop the ingredients, and smash with a knife to purée.) Slowly drizzle in the olive oil, and add the Parmesan, mixing well to incorporate. Season with lemon juice and salt, to taste, just before serving.

3 tablespoons pine nuts
2–3 garlic cloves, peeled and finely chopped (about 1 tablespoon)
½ cup chopped fresh mint leaves
¼ cup chopped fresh Italian parsley leaves
1 teaspoon kosher salt
½ cup extra-virgin olive oil
¼ cup (1 ounce) finely grated Parmigiano-Reggiano
2–3 teaspoons fresh lemon juice

Parsley Basil Pesto

Preheat the oven to 325 degrees.

Spread the pine nuts on a baking sheet, and toast in the oven for about 8–10 minutes, until lightly browned.

3 tablespoons pine nuts
2–3 garlic cloves, peeled and finely chopped (about 1 tablespoon)

Using a mortar and pestle, pulverize the pine nuts, garlic, basil, parsley, and salt into a smooth paste. (If you don't have one, finely chop the ingredients, and smash with a knife to purée.) Slowly drizzle in the olive oil, and add the Parmesan, mixing well to incorporate. Season with lemon juice and salt, to taste, just before serving.

¼ cup plus 2 tablespoons chopped fresh basil leaves

¼ cup plus 2 tablespoons chopped fresh Italian parsley leaves

1 teaspoon kosher salt

½ cup extra-virgin olive oil

¼ cup (1 ounce) finely grated Parmigiano-Reggiano

1 tablespoon fresh lemon juice, or to taste

Salsa Verde

Using a mortar and pestle, pulverize the anchovies, capers, garlic, and salt to a smooth paste. (If you don't have one, finely chop the ingredients, and smash with a knife to purée.) Add the parsley, marjoram, and mint, and continue pulverizing to break down the herbs. Slowly add the olive oil, stirring well to combine. Season with salt and lemon juice, to taste, just before serving.

3 or 4 3-inch-long salt-packed anchovies, rinsed well, backbone removed, finely chopped (about 1 tablespoon)

2 tablespoons plus ½ teaspoon capers, preferably salt-packed, rinsed well and finely chopped

3 garlic cloves, peeled and finely chopped (about 1 tablespoon)

½ teaspoon kosher salt

½ cup plus 2 tablespoons coarsely chopped fresh Italian parsley leaves

1 tablespoon plus 1½ teaspoons coarsely chopped fresh marjoram leaves

1 tablespoon plus 1½ teaspoons coarsely chopped fresh mint leaves

¾ cup extra-virgin olive oil

1–2 teaspoons fresh lemon juice

BREADS

I couldn't do a book about sandwiches without offering a few bread recipes. The truth of the matter is that these days, in any large city across the country, you can find delicious hearth-baked breads in either neighborhood bakeries or supermarkets. But if you're the type of person who has to make everything from scratch, here are some loaves that are easy to bake and go well with my toppings and fillings.

BRIOCHE LOAF

Warm the milk in a saucepan over low heat until it's just warm to the touch.

Place the yeast in the bowl of an electric mixer. Pour the milk over it, and let it soften for 1–2 minutes. Add 1 of the eggs and 1 cup of the flour, and stir by hand to combine them. Sprinkle 1 more cup of flour over the mixture, without stirring. Cover the bowl tightly with plastic wrap, and set it aside in a warm place until the surface of the flour cracks, about 30–40 minutes.

Add the sugar, salt, remaining eggs, and remaining 1½ cups of flour to the yeast mixture. Using an electric mixer fitted with the dough hook, mix on low speed for 1–2 minutes, until the ingredients are combined. Turn the mixer up to medium-high speed, and continue to mix for about 15 minutes, until the dough wraps itself around the hook and is smooth, shiny, and slightly sticky. It may be necessary to add up to another ¼ cup of flour to encourage the dough to leave the sides of the bowl.

Turn the mixer down to medium-low speed, and add the butter, a few tablespoons at a time. After all of the butter has been added, turn the mixer up to medium-high, and beat the dough for about 2–3 more minutes, until the dough wraps itself around the dough hook. If necessary, add more flour to encourage the dough to leave the sides of the bowl. The dough will be smooth, shiny, and sticky, but not oily.

Transfer the dough to a lightly floured work surface. Clean the mixing bowl, and lightly coat it with vegetable oil. Return the dough to the oiled bowl, cover it tightly with plastic wrap, and set it aside in a warm place until the dough has doubled in size, about 2 to 2½ hours.

Spread the dough onto a floured, parchment-lined baking sheet. Dust the surface of the dough with flour, cover it with parchment paper, and refrigerate it for 6–8 hours.

Brush 2 6-cup-capacity (8½-by-4½-by-2½-inch) Pyrex or ceramic loaf pans with the melted butter. Or, if you are making tea sandwiches, use 1 12-cup-capacity (12½-by-4-by-4-inch) pullman-style metal loaf pan brushed with melted butter.

Remove the dough from the refrigerator, and take off the top piece of

⅓ cup whole milk

¾ ounce (1 tablespoon) packed fresh cake yeast, or 2¾ teaspoons active dry yeast

6 extra-large eggs

3½–3¾ cups unbleached all-purpose flour, plus extra for dusting

⅓ cup sugar

1 teaspoon kosher salt

2 sticks (8 ounces) unsalted butter, softened but not greasy

Vegetable oil, for coating the bowl

1 tablespoon melted butter, for brushing the pans

1 egg yolk, lightly beaten with a few drops of water, for brushing the loaves

parchment paper. Turn the dough out onto a lightly floured work surface, and remove the bottom piece of parchment paper. Cut the dough in half, squaring off the edges to maintain its rectangular shape.

Working with one piece of dough at a time, lightly dust the top with flour. Using the palm of your hands, and flouring your hands and dough as necessary, flatten the dough into an 8-by-10-inch rectangle, patting it to an even thickness. Fold the left and right sides over to meet in the middle. Press down firmly on the seam to seal and square off the edges. Fold the bottom edge up to the middle and, using the heel of your hand dipped in flour, press down firmly to seal the seam. Do the same with the top edge, bringing it down to meet in the middle and seal. Bring the top edge to the bottom edge, pressing down firmly to seal the seam. Tuck in the ends on the left and right sides, pressing down firmly to seal the edges.

Turn the dough seam side up. Working with one hand on top of the other and palms down, begin to roll the dough from the center outward. As the dough starts to stretch, uncross your hands and continue rolling with light, even pressure, moving your hands all the way to the ends, until the cylinder is 8 inches long, the same length as your pan. (Or, for the tea sandwiches, roll the cylinder to 12 inches long.)

Place the dough, seam side down, in the prepared pan. Make a fist and, using the flat surface of your knuckles, knock down the dough from end to end, so that it spreads evenly and covers the surface of the pan.

Repeat with the other half of dough.

Brush both loaves with the egg, and place the pans on a baking sheet. Place the baking sheet in a large plastic garbage bag, and blow into the bag to create a dome of air that will allow room for the dough to rise. Set aside in a warm place, and allow the dough to rise for about 2 hours, until the loaves are tripled in size or have risen about $\frac{1}{2}$ inch above the pans.

About $\frac{1}{2}$ hour before the loaves have finished rising, adjust the oven rack to the middle position, and preheat the oven to 375 degrees.

Bake the loaves for 1 hour and 10 minutes, until they're nicely browned on all sides. Remove them from the oven, and knock one of the pans against the counter to release the loaf. To make sure the bread is done, tap your finger on the side of the loaf. If the bread is done, it will be very firm. (If the loaf is still soft, it will collapse; return it to the pan, and continue to bake in the oven for another 5–10 minutes.) Remove both loaves from the pans, and cool them completely. Wrap them tightly in plastic. If you're not going to use the bread that day, freeze it until you're ready.

YIELD: 1 12½-by-4-by-4-inch pullman-style loaf or 2 8½-by-4½-by-2½-inch loaves

CRUSTY WHITE LOAF

This basic Crusty White Loaf yields the closest-tasting bread to a homemade or store-bought sourdough loaf possible without the project of a sourdough starter. The dough is very wet and sticky and needs to be baked in a loaf pan, which unfortunately won't yield a slice of bread the same size as from a larger, 2-pound oval loaf. Since these slices will be a little smaller, adapt them to the recipes in the book by using six slices for open-faced sandwiches or twelve slices for the closed-faced ones. For the open-faced sandwiches, cut the bread in half on the diagonal after grilling, and serve each person three slices with the appropriate amounts of toppings or fillings.

This recipe will make either two small crusty loaves, twelve pan-bagna rolls, eighteen odds & ends rolls, or about forty-five snackbreads.

TO MAKE THE SPONGE: You must start the sponge 8 to 12 hours ahead.

Stir the dissolved yeast mixture well, measure out 2 tablespoons, and pour it into a large mixing bowl. Discard the remaining yeast mixture.

Add the 1½ cups of water to the bowl, and whisk to combine. Add the flour, and stir to incorporate it. Cover the bowl tightly with plastic wrap. Allow the mixture to sit for 8 to 12 hours at room temperature, until the surface has domed slightly and is bubbly, lumpy, and shiny.

TO MAKE THE DOUGH: Place the sponge mixture, 2¼ cups of water, yeast, and flour in the bowl of an electric mixer fitted with the dough hook,

FOR THE SPONGE

1¼ teaspoons (0.3 ounce) packed fresh yeast, or 1⅛ teaspoons (½ packet) active dry yeast, dissolved in 2 cups cool water (about 75 degrees)

1½ cups cool water (about 75 degrees)

2½ cups plus 2 tablespoons bread flour

FOR THE DOUGH

2¼ cups cool water (about 75 degrees)

1¼ teaspoons (0.3 ounces) packed fresh yeast, or 1⅛ teaspoons (½ packet) active dry yeast

4¾ cups plus 2 tablespoons bread flour

1 tablespoon plus 2 teaspoons kosher salt

Vegetable oil, for coating the bowl

and mix on low for 2 minutes, until the ingredients are partially combined. Add the salt, turn the mixer up to medium, and mix for 2 minutes. Turn the mixer to medium high, and mix for another 4 minutes. (The dough will be very wet and seem more like a batter, but it will get easier to work with by the end of its 4 rises.)

Pour the dough out onto a well-floured surface. Clean the mixing bowl, and coat it lightly with vegetable oil. Holding the bowl just below the edge of the floured surface, use a rubber spatula to scrape the dough back into the bowl. Cover tightly with plastic wrap. Set it aside in a warm place, and allow the dough to rise for 30–45 minutes, until it's slightly domed and bubbly.

Pour the dough out onto a well-floured surface. Roughly square off the edges, and fold each of the 4 sides of the dough in on itself, toward the center, being careful not to deflate it. Scrape the dough back into the bowl, and cover tightly with plastic wrap. Set it aside in a warm place, and allow the dough to rise for another 30–45 minutes, until it's slightly domed. Repeat the process 2 more times, for a total of 4 rises and 3 folds.

For the Crusty Loaves

TO SHAPE THE LOAVES: Brush 2 6-cup-capacity (8½-by-4½-by-2½-inch) glass Pyrex loaf pans with melted butter.

Turn the dough out onto a heavily floured work surface, and cut it in half. Fold each of the 4 sides of one of the halves in on itself, toward the center, being careful not to deflate it. Continue folding in this manner until the dough is the size of the loaf pans.

Place the dough, seam side down, in the prepared pan.

Repeat with the other half of the dough. Place the loaf pans on a baking sheet and place inside of a large plastic garbage bag, and blow air into the bag to create a dome of air that will allow room for the dough to rise. Set aside in a warm place, and allow the dough to rise for 30–40 minutes, until it's domed.

About ½ hour before the loaves have finished rising, adjust the oven rack to the middle position, and preheat the oven to 500 degrees.

Just before baking, toss a few cups of ice into the oven and close the door to create steam. Turn the oven down to 450 degrees. Place the loaf pans in the oven, a few inches apart. Bake for 15 minutes, and remove them from the oven.

Turn the loaves out of the pan by turning them upside down onto the work surface. Return the loaves (right side up, without pans) to the oven, spaced a few inches apart on the oven rack, to finish baking another 30 minutes. To make sure the bread is done, tap your finger against the bottom of the loaves. If the bread is done, you will hear a hollow sound. Remove them from the oven, and cool completely.

YIELD: 2 loaves

FOR THE PAN BAGNA OR ODDS & ENDS FOCACCETE ROLLS

Adjust the oven rack to the middle position, and preheat the oven to 500 degrees.

Pour the dough onto a well-floured surface and divide the dough into 12 4-inch-diameter pieces. Or, if you're making the *focaccete,* divide into 18 2-inch-diameter pieces. Transfer them carefully by scooping them up with floured fingertips onto 2 parchment-lined baking sheets, spacing them at least 2 inches apart. Gently shape each piece into a rounded shape, by cupping your floured hands around them. Set the baking sheets aside in a warm place, and allow the dough to rise for about 20 minutes.

Flatten each roll by dimpling it firmly with your fingers. Keep in mind these are rustic, free-form shapes.

Just before baking, toss a few cups of ice into the oven and close the door to create steam. Turn the oven down to 450 degrees, and bake the buns until they're a light golden brown, about 30 minutes.

YIELD: 12 pan-bagna or 18 *focaccete* rolls

Tea Sandwich Loaf

Place the water, yeast, flour, powdered milk, and sugar in the bowl of an electric mixer fitted with a dough hook. Mix on low speed for a few seconds, just until the ingredients are incorporated. Turn the mixer up to medium speed, and mix for 2 more minutes. The dough should come together and not stick to the sides of the bowl. Turn the mixer off, and add the salt. Mix on low speed to combine. Turn the mixer up to medium speed, add the softened butter, and continue mixing for another 8–10 minutes, until the dough is smooth and elastic.

Remove the dough from the bowl, place it on a lightly floured work surface, and knead it for a few minutes by hand. Clean the mixing bowl, and lightly coat it with vegetable oil. Return the dough to the oiled bowl, cover it tightly with plastic wrap, and set aside in a warm place until the dough has doubled in size, about 45 minutes.

Turn the dough out onto a lightly floured work surface and dust the top with flour. Pat it with the palms of your hands lightly to deflate it. Tuck the edges under, cover it with a kitchen towel, and allow it to rest for about 15 minutes.

Brush a 12-cup-capacity (12½-by-4-by-4-inch) pullman-style metal loaf pan with the melted butter.

Using the palms of your hands, and flouring your hands and dough as necessary, flatten the dough into an 8-by-10-inch rectangle, patting it to an even thickness. Fold the left and right sides over to meet in the middle. Press down firmly on the seam to seal it and square off the edges. Fold the bottom edge up to the middle and, using the heel of your hand dipped in flour, press down firmly to seal. Fold the top edge down to meet in the middle, and press down firmly with the heel of your hand to seal. Bring the top edge to the bottom edge again, pressing down firmly to seal the seam. Tuck in the ends on the left and right sides, pressing down firmly to seal.

Turn the dough seam side up. Working hand over hand with your palms down, begin to roll the dough from the center outward. As the dough starts to stretch, uncross your hands and continue rolling with light, even pres-

1⅓ cups lukewarm water
2½ teaspoons (0.6 ounce) packed fresh yeast, or 2¼ teaspoons (1 packet) active dry yeast
3¾ cups plus 1 tablespoon unbleached bread flour, plus extra for dusting
1 tablespoon powdered milk
1 tablespoon plus 1 teaspoon sugar
2 teaspoons kosher salt
3 tablespoons unsalted butter, softened, but not greasy
Vegetable oil, for coating the bowl
1 tablespoon melted butter, for brushing the loaf pan

sure, moving your hands all the way to the ends of the dough, until the cylinder is about 12 inches long, almost the same length as your pan.

Place the loaf, seam side down, in the prepared pan. With one hand formed into a fist, using the flat surface of your knuckles, knock down the dough from end to end so that it spreads evenly and covers the surface of the pan. Place the loaf pan on a baking sheet and place it inside of a large plastic garbage bag, and blow air into the bag, to create a dome of air that will allow room for the dough to rise. Set aside in a warm place, and allow the dough to rise for about $1\frac{1}{2}$ hours, until the loaf has tripled in size and risen $\frac{1}{2}$ inch above the rim of the pan.

About $\frac{1}{2}$ hour before the loaf has finished rising, adjust the oven rack to the lower position, and preheat the oven to 500 degrees.

Just before baking, turn the oven down to 475 degrees. Bake the loaf for 50 minutes, until it's a light golden brown, rotating the pan halfway through baking.

Remove from the oven, and knock the pan against a counter to release the loaf. To make sure the bread is done, tap your finger on the side of the loaf. If it's done, it will be very firm. (If not, return the loaf to the pan, and continue baking for another 5 minutes or so.) Remove from the pan, and cool completely.

YIELD: 1 2-pound pullman-style sandwich loaf

HOT DOG BUNS

This recipe makes more buns than you'll need for the Fried Oyster Sandwich recipe on page 95. You can cut this recipe in half or freeze the extras or, even better yet, throw some dogs on the grill.

1 cup plus 2 tablespoons whole milk

1 tablespoon plus 1 teaspoon
(1 ounce) packed fresh yeast,
or 1 tablespoon active dry yeast

¼ cup sugar

3¾ cups plus 2 tablespoons
unbleached all-purpose flour,
plus extra for dusting

2 extra-large eggs, lightly beaten

1 tablespoon kosher salt

3 tablespoons unsalted butter,
softened but not greasy

Vegetable oil, for coating the bowl

In a small saucepan, warm the milk over medium heat until it's just warm to the touch.

Place the yeast, sugar, and flour in the bowl of an electric mixer fitted with the dough hook, and pour the milk over it. Mix on low speed for about 2 minutes, until the ingredients are combined.

Measure out ⅓ cup of the eggs, and discard the rest.

Add the eggs and salt to the bowl, and mix on high speed for about 4–5 minutes, until the dough is smooth and shiny. Turn the mixer down to medium speed, add the butter in small pieces, turn the mixer up to high speed, and mix 1 more minute, until the butter is incorporated.

Turn the dough out onto a lightly floured work surface, and knead it a few times to gather it into a ball. Clean the mixing bowl, and lightly coat it with vegetable oil. Return the dough to the oiled bowl, cover it tightly with plastic wrap, and set it aside in a warm place until the dough has doubled in size, about 1–1½ hours.

Turn the dough out gently onto a floured work surface. With the palms of your hands, flatten the dough slightly and stretch to elongate it into an 18-inch log. Cut the dough into 10 pieces, and place them on a lightly floured surface, 1 inch apart. Cover them with a kitchen towel, and allow them to rest for 10 minutes.

Working with one piece at a time (keeping the rest of the pieces covered), place the dough on a lightly floured work surface. Using the palm of your hands, and flouring your hand and dough as necessary, flatten the dough into a 4-inch rectangle, patting it to an even thickness.

Working quickly and using as little flour as possible, fold the left and right sides of the rectangle over to meet in the middle. Press down firmly on the seam with the heel of your hand or your fingertips, to seal it and square off the edges. Fold the bottom edge up to the middle, and press down firmly to seal the seam. Fold the top edge down to meet in the middle, and press down firmly with the heel of your hand or fingertips to seal. Bring the top edge to the bottom edge, pressing down firmly to seal. Tuck in both ends, and press down firmly to get a clean seal.

Turn the dough seam side up. Working hand over hand with your palms down, begin to roll the dough from the center outward. As the dough starts to stretch, uncross your hands and continue rolling with light, even pressure, moving your hands all the way to the ends, until the cylinder is 7 inches long and about $1\frac{1}{2}$ inches wide.

Place the dough, seam side down, on a parchment-lined baking sheet. Continue in the same manner with the remaining pieces, placing them 2 inches apart on the baking sheet. Place the baking sheet in a large plastic garbage bag, and blow air into the bag to create a dome of air that will allow room for the dough to rise. Set aside in a warm place, and allow the dough to rise for about 45 minutes to an hour, until it's spongy to the touch.

About $\frac{1}{2}$ hour before the loaf has finished rising, adjust the oven rack to the lower position and preheat the oven to 500 degrees.

Just before baking, toss a few cups of ice into the oven and close the door to create steam. Turn the oven down to 450 degrees, and bake the buns until they're a deep golden brown, about 25–30 minutes.

YIELD: 10 buns

SOURCES

For convenient mail-order shopping, here is a list of sources with websites and catalogues that provide excellent specialty products. Be sure to check your local specialty stores, well-stocked supermarkets, and gourmet delis as well.

PANINI GRILLS

Sur La Table
84 Pine Street
Seattle, Washington 98101
1-800-243-0852
www.surlatable.com

Williams-Sonoma
P.O. Box 7456
San Francisco, California 94120
1-800-541-2233
www.williams-sonoma.com

Pasquini
1501 W. Olympic Blvd.
Los Angeles, California 90015
1-213-739-8826
pasquini@pasquini.com

QUALITY INGREDIENTS (SUCH AS CHEESES, CURED MEATS, OLIVE OILS, VINEGARS, FLEUR DE SEL, ROASTED RED PEPPERS, BEANS, OLIVES, PESTOS, CAPER BERRIES, ARTICHOKES, BACCALÀ, CRYSTALLIZED SUGAR, COCOA NIBS, AND OTHER SPECIALTY ITEMS)

Arthur Avenue Caterers
2344 Arthur Avenue
Bronx, New York 10458
1-866-272-5264

Balducci's
424 Sixth Avenue
New York, New York 10011
1-800-225-3822
www.balducci.com

Chef Shop
www.chefshop.com

Corti Brothers
1-800-509-3663

Dean & DeLuca
2525 East Thirty-sixth North Circle
Wichita, Kansas 67219
1-800-221-7714
Main Store:
560 Broadway
New York, New York 10012
1-212-226-6800
www.dean-deluca.com

Formaggio Kitchen, Inc.
244 Huron Avenue
Cambridge, Massachusetts 02138
1-888-212-3224
www.formaggiokitchen.com

Grateful Palate
1-888-472-5283
www.gratefulpalate.com

Ideal Cheese Shop
1205 Second Avenue
New York, New York 10021
1-800-480-2426
www.idealcheese.com

King Arthur Flour
Norwich, Vermont
1-800-827-6836
www.kingarthurflour.com

La Espagnola
25020 Doble Avenue
Harbor City, California 90710
1-310-539-0455
www.donajuana.com

Manicaretti (They don't sell retail;
however, they list a directory on their
website that includes an extensive list
of places to purchase their products.)
www.manicaretti.com

Murray's Cheese Shop
257 Bleecker Street
New York, New York 10014
1-888-692-4339
www.murrayscheese.com

Oakville Grocery
7856 St. Helena
Oakville, California 94562
1-800-736-6602
www.oakvillegrocery.com

The Pasta Shop
5655 College Avenue
Oakland, California 94618
1-510-547-4005
www.rockridgemarkethall.com

Pasta Works
3735 SE Hawthorne Blvd.
Portland, Oregon 97214
1-503-232-1010
www.pastaworks.com

The Spanish Table
1427 Western Avenue
Seattle, Washington 98101
1-206-682-2827
or
1814 San Pablo Avenue
Berkeley, California 94702
1-510-548-1383
www.spanishtable.com

Surfas
8825 National Blvd.
Culver City, California 90232
1-310-559-4770
www.surfasonline.com

Vino e Olio
1-877-846-6365
www.vinoeolio.com

Whole Foods Markets
(located across the country)
1-888-945-3637
www.wholefoods.com

Williams-Sonoma
P.O. Box 7456
San Francisco, California 94120
1-800-541-2233
www.williams-sonoma.com

Zabar's
2245 Broadway
New York, New York 10024
1-800-697-6301
www.zabars.com

Zingerman's
422 Detroit Street
Ann Arbor, Michigan 48104
1-888-636-8162
www.zingermans.com

ACKNOWLEDGMENTS

When Sandwich Night first began five years ago, our menu consisted of just a few items written out on a tiny chalkboard that we'd prop up behind the bar. Below are just some of the many people who helped me turn this idea into what *Los Angeles Magazine* declared "One of the 10 Reasons Not to Leave Los Angeles."

To Thursday night sous-chef, Caryl Lee Kim, who is as reliably meticulous as she is tardy, and who likes to think that she just butters the bread. In fact, she makes the best Croque Madame and Croque Monsieur. She keeps me organized (not to mention her two food-runner "husbands," Juanito Bautista and Tomas Martinez). Hopefully, Caryl Lee, you do not regret the day you innocently asked, "Is there any way I can help you around the kitchen?"

Besides helping me brainstorm and formulate recipes, each week chefs Chris Kidder, Dan Trudeau, and Matt Molina prepare all the components that free me to make as many different kinds of sandwiches as I can think of. Without them, we'd still be at the three-items-written-on-a-tiny-chalkboard phase.

Sandwich Night is a lot more complicated than just Caryl and me and our sandwich presses. What our customers don't see are line cooks Marcella Mora, Melissa Kelly, and Shelly Heyward, and my daughter Vanessa in the back of the kitchen, frying french fries, tossing salads, and poaching eggs, and to them, I am especially grateful.

To my pastry chef, Kim Boyce, and her crew—Dahlia "Dolly" Narvaez, Roxanna "Roxy" Quiros, and Elizabeth Belkind. Each night, including Sandwich Night at Campanile, the pastry department comes up with wonderful desserts to end the meal. Many thanks go out to them for testing, testing, and retesting every sweet in the dessert chapter of this book. If you don't understand anything about any of these recipes, call them, not me.

To everyone who tirelessly puts up with the added chaos of Thursday night—the maître d', hostesses, bartenders, wait staff, and table stewards.

To my recipe testers—led by the multitalented Jessica Buonocore—Jack Stumpf, Paul Schrade, and Teri Gelber.

To Leyla Aker, whom I've never met (or seen). You line-edited my text and made sure that I got the book I wanted. I'd love to meet you someday!

To the photographer, Amy Neunsinger, who made all of my sandwiches (and desserts) look as good as they're supposed to taste.

To my editor, Peter Gethers, who didn't blink an eye when I floated out the idea of a book on . . . *sandwiches*. And to my agent, Janice Donnaud, who was able to sell the concept exactly as I saw it.

My thanks go out to all the journalists who really helped spread the word: Meredith Brody, Margot Dougherty, Jonathan Gold, Michelle Huneven, Laurie Ochoa, Ruth Reichl, and S. Irene Virbila.

To my best friend, Margy Rochlin, who was a Sandwich Night booster from day one and who always showed up with a gigantic crowd of friends. Margy, thanks for pushing aside your own work and accepting the responsibility of e-mail correspondence and research.

To writer Teri Gelber (pronounced Gel-BURR), who worked incredibly hard on this book. Every day, you sat alongside me at the Campanile bar with your laptop and managed to turn my babbling into prose. Teri, we did another one! (And by the way, everything really wasn't your fault . . .).

INDEX

CREDITS

Thanks to the following shops for lending us such nice things:

OK
8303 W. Third Street
Los Angeles, California 90048
okstore@aol.com

Fitzsu Society 01
7970 Melrose Avenue
Los Angeles, California 90046
www.fitzsu.com

Soolip Bungalow
548 Norwich Drive
Los Angeles, California 90048

Chestnuts & Papayas
459½ S. La Brea Avenue
Los Angeles, California 90036
www.chesnutsandpapayas.com

Arp
8311½ W. Third Street
Los Angeles, California 90048

Shelter
7920 Beverly Blvd.
Los Angeles, California 90048

Armani Casa
157 N. Robertson Blvd.
Los Angeles, California 90048

Sur La Table
Santa Monica Store
www.surlatable.com

A NOTE ABOUT THE AUTHORS

Nancy Silverton owns and operates, with her husband, Mark Peel, Campanile restaurant (recipient of the 2001 James Beard Award for Best Restaurant) and the La Brea Bakery in Los Angeles. She is the author of *Nancy Silverton's Pastries from the La Brea Bakery* (recipient of a 2000 *Food & Wine* Best Cookbook Award), *Nancy Silverton's Breads from the La Brea Bakery,* and *Desserts.* She is also the coauthor, with Mark Peel, of *Mark Peel and Nancy Silverton at Home* and *The Food of Campanile.* She lives in Los Angeles with her husband and their three children.

Teri Gelber is a food writer and public-radio producer living and eating well in Los Angeles.

A NOTE ON THE TYPE

This book was set in Diotima, a light roman typeface designed by Gudrun Zapf–von Hesse, a largely self-taught lettering artist. Her husband, Hermann Zapf, the most widely known type designer in the world, has often had to explain to fellow typesetters that it is not one of his types, but rather his wife's design. Introduced by the Stempel Foundry in Frankfurt am Main in 1954, Diotima has since attracted the attention of those typographers with a fondness for classical printing types. Reminiscent of the splendid proportions of the lettering on the monument to Trajan in Rome, which for nineteen hundred years has been the inspiration for majuscule lettering, the capitals of the font are particularly distinguished. Among the other typefaces Gudrun Zapf–von Hesse has designed are Smaragd, a set of outline capitals with hairline serifs, and Ariadne, a set of flowing italic initials.

COMPOSED BY NORTH MARKET STREET GRAPHICS, LANCASTER, PENNSYLVANIA

PRINTED AND BOUND BY BUTLER AND TANNER LTD., FROME, ENGLAND

DESIGNED BY IRIS WEINSTEIN